Student Name: _____

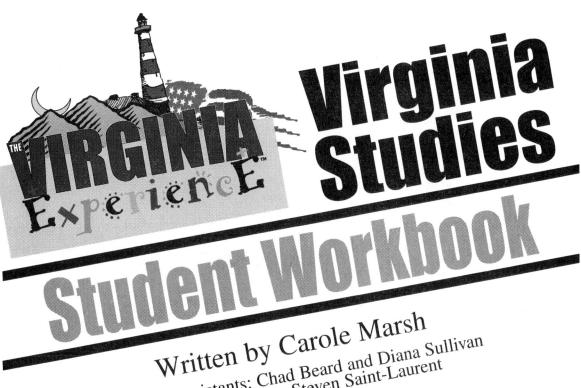

Virginia Studies
Student Workbook

Written by Carole Marsh

Editorial Assistants: Chad Beard and Diana Sullivan
Graphic Designer: Steven Saint-Laurent

NEW EDITION!
Current Standards
Test scores have increased as much as 400%

The Virginia Experience

Published by

GALLOPADE™
INTERNATIONAL

800-536-2GET
www.gallopade.com

ISBN 0-635-01046-1

Gallopade is proud to be a member of the National Council for the Social Studies,
as well as these educational organizations and associations:

Carole Marsh Virginia Titles

Virginia Experience Grade-Specific Readers—Famous People in the SOL

Addams, Jane
Anthony, Susan B.
Appleseed, Johnny
Ashe, Arthur
Byrd, Harry Flood
Brown, John
Cabot, John
Cartier, Jacques
Carver, George Washington
Champlain, Samuel de
Crockett, Davy
Columbus, Christopher
Franklin, Benjamin
Grant, Ulysses S.
Henry, Patrick
Jackson, Thomas "Stonewall"
James I, King
Jefferson, Thomas
Jones, John Paul
Keller, Helen
King, Martin Luther, Jr.
Lafayette, Marquis de
Lee, Robert E.
Lincoln, Abraham
Madison, James
Marshall, Thurgood
Mason, George
Monroe, James
Newport, Christopher
Parks, Rosa
Ponce de Leon, Juan
Pocahontas
Powell Jr., Lewis F.
Powhatan, Chief
Revere, Paul
Rolfe, John
Robinson, Jackie
Ross, Betsy
Smith, Captain John
Stuart, J.E.B.
Tubman, Harriet
Turner, Nat
Walker, Maggie Lena
Washington, Booker T.
Washington, George
Wilder, L. Douglas
Wilson, Woodrow
Wythe, George

The Virginia Experience Kindergarten Student Workbook
The Virginia Experience Kindergarten Teacher Resource
The Virginia Experience First Grade Student Workbook
The Virginia Experience First Grade Teacher Resource
The Virginia Experience Second Grade Student Workbook
The Virginia Experience Second Grade Teacher Resource
The Virginia Experience Third Grade Student Workbook
The Virginia Experience Third Grade Teacher Resource
The Virginia Experience Virginia Studies Workbook
The Virginia Experience Virginia Studies Teacher Resource
The Virginia Experience United States History I Workbook
The Virginia Experience United States History I Teacher Resource
The Virginia Experience United States History II Workbook
The Virginia Experience United States History II Teacher Resource
The Virginia Experience Standards of Learning Reference Guide
The Virginia Experience Poster/Map
The Virginia Experience Civics for Teachers
The Virginia Experience Economics for Teachers
20 Ways to Teach the SOL with PIZZAZZ!
A Virginia Mystery Musical!
The Virginia Experience Tee Shirt
The Virginia Experience Pencils
The Virginia Experience Biographies Book—All the Famous People in the SOL
Pass The Test! CD-ROM Kindergarten—Social Studies
Pass The Test! CD-ROM First Grade—Social Studies
Pass The Test! CD-ROM Second Grade—Social Studies
Pass The Test! CD-ROM Third Grade—Social Studies
Pass The Test! CD-ROM Virginia Studies
Virginia Facts & Factivities! CD-ROM (Lesson Plans, Reproducible Activities, & Teacher's Guide also available)
Let's Discover Virginia! CD-ROM
The BIG Virginia Reproducible Activity Book
My First Book About Virginia!
Virginia Jeopardy!: Answers & Questions About Our State
Virginia "Jography!": A Fun Run Through Our State
My First Pocket Guide: Virginia
The Very Virginia Coloring Book
Virginia Stickers
Virginia Biography Bingo Game
Virginia Geography Bingo Game
Virginia History Bingo Game

A Word from the Author...

Dear Students,

Whether you're first studying the great state of Virginia, or reviewing for your Standards of Learning test, I have a secret for you: almost everything you ever want or need to know, you can learn right in your own backyard . . . in your very own state!

As you progress in school, you will find that your Virginia state studies prepare you to understand people and places around the world. Why? Because you will already possess a wealth of knowledge about how things work – history, geography, politics, etc. – in a single corner of the world that you know well: your own state!

Virginia is a very special state to study. It has a history so remarkable that it is impossible to successfully study the past (or the present!) without understanding that what happened in Virginia helped create the greatest nation on earth – America! Virginia enjoys an amazing geography of incredible beauty and fascination. The state's people are unique and have accomplished many great things. When you learn about these extraordinary people, you will learn about yourself!

Almost everything about Virginia is interesting – whether that's politics, sea life, mountain heritage, surprising trivia, the arts, legend and lore – and much, much more. Even people who have long been out of school and who could read about and study any subject they desire (and who don't even have to pass a test!) are drawn to study your state – The Commonwealth of Virginia.

I have learned a lot by researching, writing, and photographing The Virginia Experience books and other products. So come along with me and enjoy your very own Virginia Experience – it's the trip of a lifetime!

Carole Marsh

Table of Contents

Icon Identification 6

Section I ~ Virginia: The Land and Its First Inhabitants 7

Chapter 1 9

Section II ~ Colonization and Conflict 31

Chapter 2 33

Chapter 3 53

Chapter 4 72

Section III ~ Political Growth and Western Expansion 91

Chapter 5 93

Section IV ~ Civil War and Post-War Eras 105

Chapter 6 107

Chapter 7 118

Section V ~ Virginia: 1900 to the Present 130

Chapter 8 132

Chapter 9 143

Section VI ~ Extra Credit 155

Practice Tests 165

Section VII ~ Appendix 171

History Glossary 183

Virginia Basic Facts 180

Glossaries 182

Maps 185

Index 190

About the Author / Notes About Answer Key 192

Icon Identification

Hard-To-Believe-But-True!
Fascinating trivia!

Map Skill Builder
Learn map skills and never be lost!

Question for Discussion
Who wants to be a millionaire?!

Reading Activity
The best kind of activity!

Scavenger Hunt!
Stuff for you to look for!

Math Experience
A neat math problem or info!

Quick Quiz
Think fast!

Special Economics Info
Money Makes the World Go 'Round

Origin/Definition
Word origins or definitions.

The Great Debate
A chance to share your opinion!

Background Check
Deep digging unearthed this stuff!

Look-It-Up!
We can't give you EVERYTHING!

Enrichment
Stuff that will stick with you!

High Tech
Computer Technology Connections!

Special Civics Information

Quick Review
You didn't forget, did you?

Write About It!
A writing activity.

Scratch Pad
A place for calculations... or doodles!

One More - Just for Fun!
All work and no play...

Essential Skills
You can't live without these!

Section 1

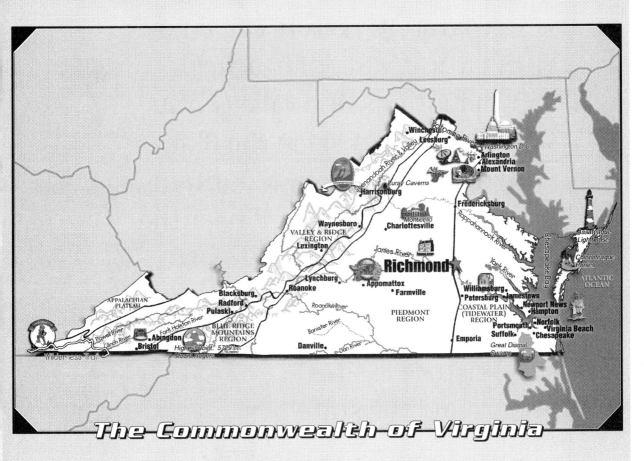

The Commonwealth of Virginia

Virginia:
The Land and its First Inhabitants

Thanks to Virginia's varied geography, visitors can enjoy the beauty of beaches, mountains, and valleys. You can hike or ski in the Blue Ridge or Allegheny Mountains, swim or sun yourself near the Atlantic Ocean, and learn about our nation's history by visiting the many historical sites around the state!

Chapter 1

VS.2a — Map tools and skills help us find our way around Virginia and the world! Correlates with VS.1i.

Map Skills!

We use a map to find the *relative location* of a place. You can determine where a place is by looking to see what other places it is near. For example, Virginia is bordered by two large bodies of water: the Chesapeake Bay and the Atlantic Ocean. Virginia also borders these states: Maryland, West Virginia, Kentucky, Tennessee, and North Carolina.

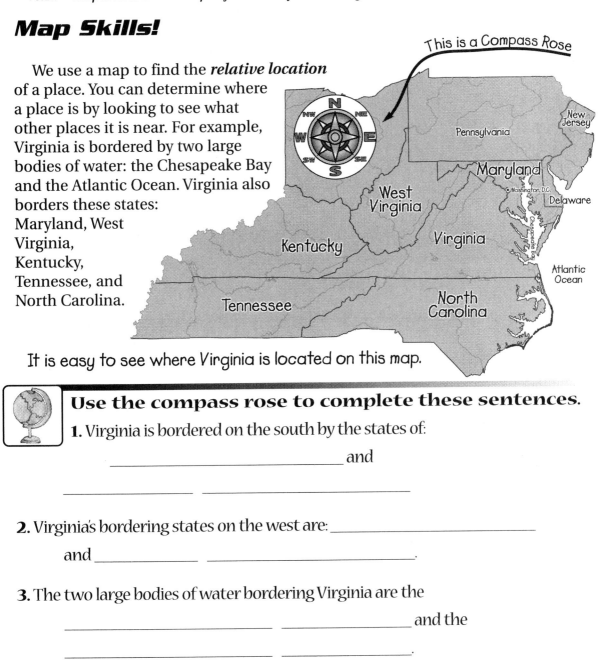

This is a Compass Rose

It is easy to see where Virginia is located on this map.

Use the compass rose to complete these sentences.

1. Virginia is bordered on the south by the states of:

_____ and

_____ _____

2. Virginia's bordering states on the west are: _____

and _____ _____.

3. The two large bodies of water bordering Virginia are the

_____ _____ and the

_____ _____.

On this map, can you find the state of Virginia, just by looking at some of the places it is near?

If so, write its name on the state.

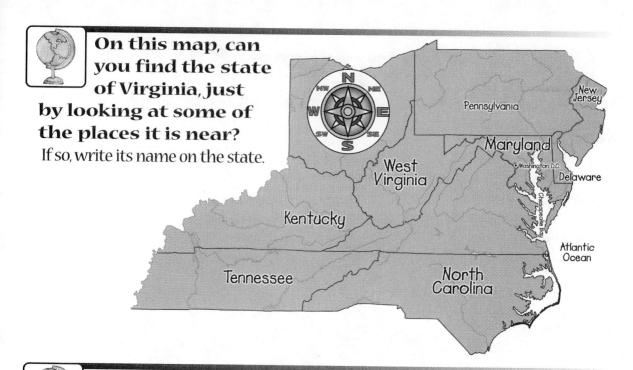

Virginia is one of the 50 United States. Here is a map of the United States.

Label the state of Virginia with its postal abbreviation, VA.

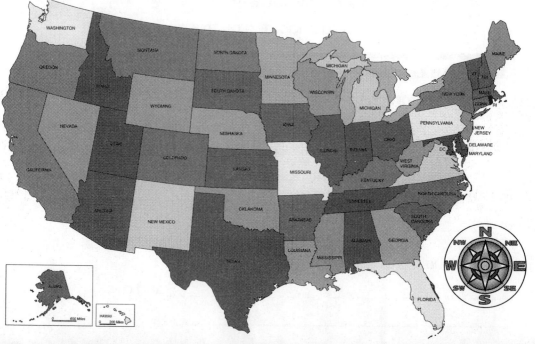

Virginia was one of the thirteen original states.

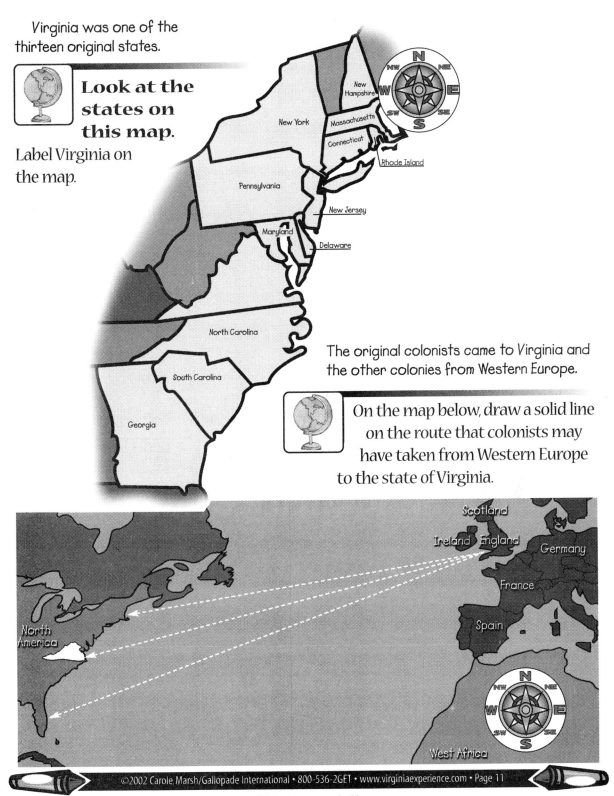

Look at the states on this map.

Label Virginia on the map.

New Hampshire

New York

Massachusetts

Connecticut

Rhode Island

Pennsylvania

New Jersey

Maryland

Delaware

North Carolina

South Carolina

Georgia

The original colonists came to Virginia and the other colonies from Western Europe.

On the map below, draw a solid line on the route that colonists may have taken from Western Europe to the state of Virginia.

Scotland

Ireland England

Germany

France

Spain

North America

West Africa

Virginia's Five Regions!

Virginia is divided into five geographic regions. These are:

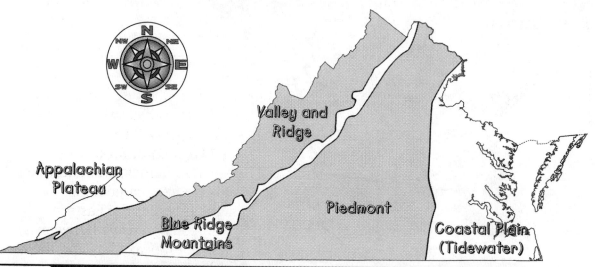

 Geographic regions have distinctive characteristics.

Region	Type of Land	Land Use
Coastal Plain (Tidewater)	Flat land, coastal plain	Vegetable & tobacco farming, fishing, shipbuilding
Piedmont	Rolling hills, plateau	Lumbering and farming
Blue Ridge Mountains	Old rounded mountains	Farming, lumbering, and tourism
Valley and Ridge	Mountains and valleys	Livestock, fruit, and poultry farming
Appalachian Plateau	High plateau	Coal mining

Have You Had Your Physical?

Each of Virginia's five regions has its own physical characteristics. Let's take a look!

The *Coastal Plain (Tidewater)* region's most prominent physical features are:
- It is a coastal plain, or flat land, beside coastal waters.
- It includes the large body of water called the Chesapeake Bay.
- The James, York, Rappahannock, and Potomac Rivers are located here.
- It includes the Eastern Shore, a peninsula between the Chesapeake Bay and the Atlantic Ocean.

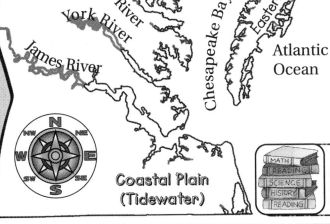

Potomac River

Rappahannock River

York River

James River

Fall Line

Chesapeake Bay

Eastern Shore

Atlantic Ocean

Coastal Plain (Tidewater)

The Fall Line: The Coastal Plain (Tidewater) and Piedmont regions of Virginia are separated by a natural border called a "fall line." This is the place where waterfalls prevent further travel on rivers.

Use the map above to complete these sentences.

1. The Coastal Plain's (Tidewater's) most prominent physical features are:

A. flat land and water   B. mountains and lakes   C. caverns and orchards

2. The Coastal Plain (Tidewater) is ___ east or ___ west of the fall line.

3. The Chesapeake is a: ___ river or ___ bay.

4. The Coastal Plain (Tidewater) is flat land beside

_____ _____.

5. The Eastern Shore is: ___ an island or ___ a peninsula.

The *Piedmont* is the area of rolling hills between the fall line and the Blue Ridge Mountains.

Rapids occur at the fall line, where rivers spill over rocky falls and onto the coastal plain to flow toward the Atlantic Ocean.

The word Piedmont means, "land at the foot of the mountains."

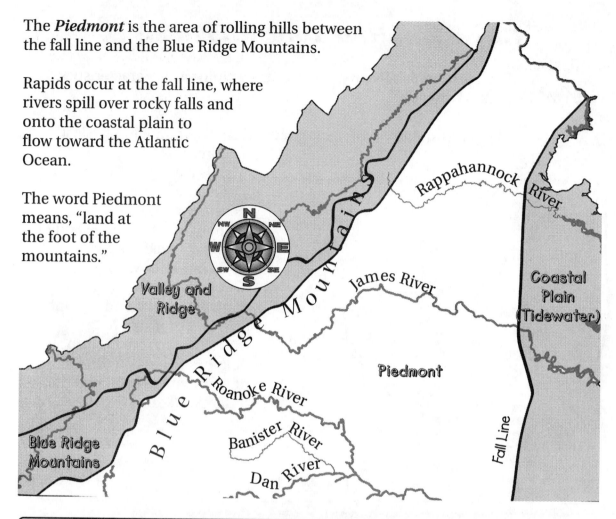

Valley and Ridge

Blue Ridge Mountains

Roanoke River

Banister River

Dan River

James River

Rappahannock River

Piedmont

Coastal Plain (Tidewater)

Fall Line

Use the map above to complete these sentences.

1. The Piedmont is ___ east or ___ west of the Fall Line.

2. A plateau is ___ higher or ___ lower than a coastal plain.

3. Rapids in the Piedmont flow ___ east or ___ west over the fall line.

4. The Piedmont region is ___ east or ___ west of the Blue Ridge Mountains.

The Blue Ridge Mountains and the Valley and Ridge regions are part of the Appalachian Mountains.

Shenandoah is what the Indians named the Blue Ridge mountains and valleys. It means "clear-eyed daughter of the stars."

The **Blue Ridge Mountains** run from Georgia, through our neighboring state of North Carolina, up into the southwestern corner of Virginia and keep going until they reach the northern tip of the state. The Blue Ridge Mountains get their name from the bluish appearance of the trees from a distance. The Blue Ridge Mountains are the source of many rivers.

Virginia's beautiful **Valley and Ridge** region is where the Appalachian Mountains and the Shenandoah River are located. Here you will find the Great Valley of Virginia and other valleys separated by ridges.

Shenandoah River

Allegheny Mountains

Appalachian Mountains

Blue Ridge Mountains

Appalachian Plateau

Valley and Ridge

Blue Ridge Mountains

Piedmont

N NE NW E W SE SW S

1. The Blue Ridge Mountains run:
_____ northeast and southwest or _____ east and west

2. The Piedmont region is _____ west or _____ east of the Blue Ridge Mountains.

3. The Blue Ridge Mountains are located between the _____ region and the Valley and Ridge region.

4. The Valley and Ridge region is located _____ east or _____ west of the Blue Ridge Mountains.

The **Appalachian Plateau** region is an area noted for its coal deposits. Only a small part of the plateau is located in Virginia.

plateau: a high land area with a flat top

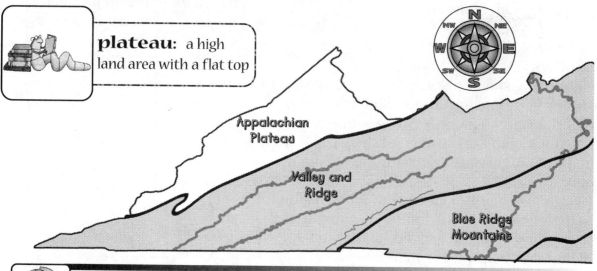

Appalachian Plateau

Valley and Ridge

Blue Ridge Mountains

Use the map to complete these sentences.

1. The Appalachian Plateau region is located in this part of Virginia:

    A. Northeast   B. Southwest   C. Southeast   D. Northwest

2. The Appalachian Plateau region is noted for its _____

_____.

3. The Appalachian Plateau region is ____ east or ____ west of the Valley and Ridge, Piedmont, and Coastal Plain (Tidewater) regions.

Black Gold

Rich deposits of coal were discovered in southwestern Virginia in the 1880s. The coalfields of southwestern Virginia are still important to the state's economy. At least 14 million tons of coal were once mined by around 4,500 miners in 300 different mines in Lee, Scott, and Wise counties. Coal is still an important Virginia natural resource.

MATH
READING
SCIENCE
HISTORY
READING

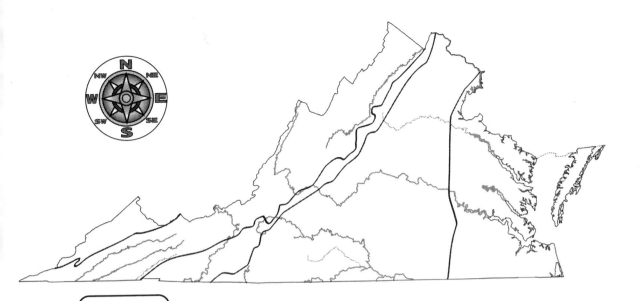

Home, Sweet Home!
Put an X where your home city, town, or county is located in Virginia.

The name of my city/town is: _____

The name of my county is: _____

I live in this region: _____

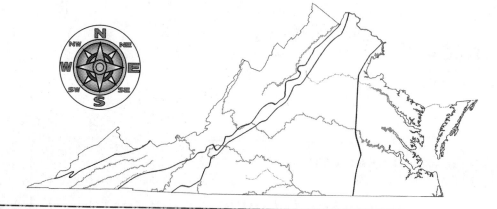

Geography Careers!
You love geography? I'm so glad! Perhaps you'd like to consider a career as one of the following:

anthropographer: *studies people and geography*
cartographer: *mapmaker*
climatologist: *studies the weather*
economic geographer: *studies resources of an area and finds locations for industries*
geographer: *studies the physical earth*
geologist: *examines rocks for earth's history*
mathematical geographer: *studies parallels and meridians*
meteorologist: *weather forecaster*
oceanographer: *studies waves, tides, and currents*
physiographer: *studies land forms*
political geographer: *plans government boundaries*

This type of geography interests me most: _____

The Development of Virginia's Cities

As Virginia grew, cities developed along the Atlantic Ocean, the Chesapeake Bay, and the state's major rivers. Geographic factors affected where cities were located and how they grew. Water features were important to the early history of Virginia.

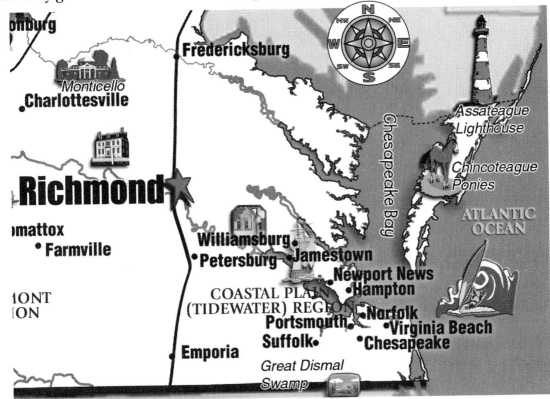

Cities developed in areas that had access to the Atlantic Ocean. The Atlantic Ocean provided transportation links between Virginia and other places such as Europe, Africa, and the Caribbean.

 Circle three cities that have access to the Atlantic Ocean.

 Circle the reasons a city might develop along the ocean:

shipping   coal mining   fishing   farming

Cities developed around the mouth of the Chesapeake Bay because of its rich natural resources and its natural harbor. The Chesapeake Bay provided a safe harbor and was a source of food and transportation for early Virginians. These cities included Norfolk, Hampton, and Yorktown.

harbor: a part of a body of water deep enough to anchor a ship

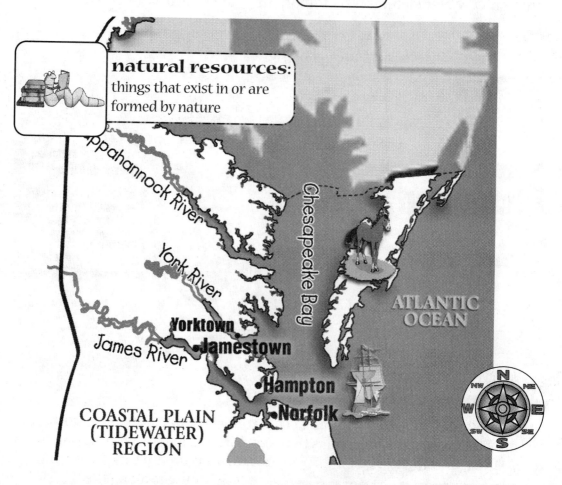

natural resources: things that exist in or are formed by nature

Rappahannock River

York River

Chesapeake Bay

ATLANTIC OCEAN

Yorktown
•Jamestown

James River

•Hampton

•Norfolk

COASTAL PLAIN (TIDEWATER) REGION

 Why did Yorktown, Hampton, and Norfolk develop around Chesapeake Bay?

_____

_____

_____

fall line: boundary between an upland region and a coastal plain

Cities developed along the fall line because it formed a natural barrier to river transportation. One example is the city of Richmond on the James River.

Label the line that some Virginia cities grew up alongside.

1. This line is called the _____ line.

2. Circle four cities that developed along the fall line.

Washington D.C.

Alexandria
Mount Vernon

Luray Caverns

Fredericksburg

Monticello

Rappahannock River

Richmond

York River

James River
Yorktown
Petersburg • Jamestown

PIEDMONT REGION

COASTAL PLAIN (TIDEWATER) REGION

Emporia

Great Dismal Swamp

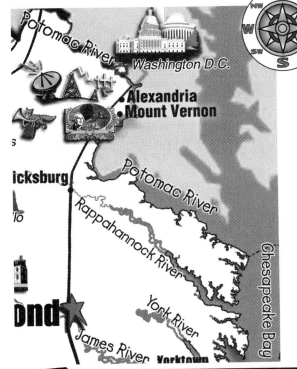

Cities developed along rivers, because rivers were the main transportation routes in early Virginia. Each river was a source of food and provided a pathway for exploration and settlement of Virginia. Alexandria is on the Potomac River; Richmond and Jamestown are on the James River; Yorktown is on the York River; and Fredericksburg is along the Rappahannock River.

Rivers flow downhill to the sea. The four major rivers that flow into the Chesapeake Bay are separated by peninsulas.

Virginia's Eastern Shore

Virginia's *Eastern Shore* is unique because:

- It is a peninsula.
- Its main industry is fishing.
- It is separated from the mainland of Virginia by the Chesapeake Bay.

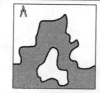 **peninsula**: a piece of land bordered by water on three sides

 Circle the land formation that is a peninsula.

A   B   C

 Why did cities like Richmond and Fredericksburg grow faster than cities that were not located on a river?

_____

_____

_____

_____

_____

_____

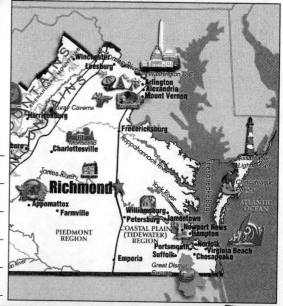

American Indians, First on Our Land!

The American Indians (First Americans) were the first people who lived in Virginia. They lived in all areas of the state. Evidence of this includes artifacts such as arrowheads, pottery, and other tools that have been found in all areas of the state. These artifacts tell a lot about the people who lived in Virginia.

There were three major American Indian language groups in Virginia.

Algonquian was spoken primarily in the Coastal Plain (Tidewater) region. The Powhatan, who met the first settlers in Jamestown, were members of this group.

Siouan was spoken primarily in the Piedmont region. The Monacan and Manahoac, who spoke the Siouan language, occupied the Piedmont region.

Iroquoian was spoken in southwestern Virginia and in southern Virginia near North Carolina. The Cherokee were a part of this group.

1. Write **I** on the region where the Iroquoian language group lived.
2. Write **S** on the region where the Siouan language group lived.
3. Write **A** on the region where the Algonquian language group lived.

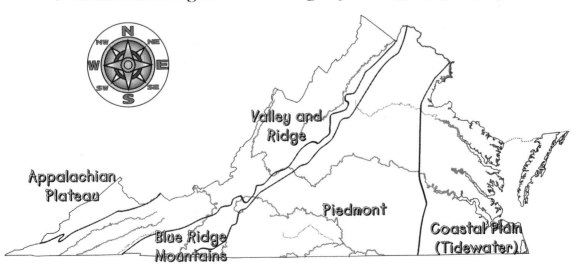

Native Americans Adapted to the Environment!

The climate in Virginia is relatively mild with distinct seasons: spring, summer, fall, and winter. The differences between the seasons result in a variety of vegetation.

> **climate**: the average weather or the regular changes in weather in a region over a period of time

Forests, which have a variety of trees, cover most of Virginia's land. Common trees include ash, beech, birch, black tupelo, hemlock, hickory, locust, maple, red cedar, spruce, sweet gum, and tulip trees. Because of Virginia's wooded landscape, Virginia Indians are referred to as Eastern Woodlands Indians.

Everything that the Indians in Virginia did, including the kinds of food they ate, the clothing they wore, and the shelters they built depended on the seasons.

FOOD

American Indian foods in Virginia changed when the seasons changed.

- Spring: Fished and picked berries
- Summer: Grew crops (beans, corn, and squash)
- Fall: Harvested crops
- Winter: Hunted birds and animals

1. What time of year did the American Indians harvest crops?

_____

2. Why do you think American Indians harvested them at this time of year?

_____

SHELTERS

American Indian shelters in Virginia were built from materials from the Indians' environment. The huts were made of bent saplings, and covered with bark and animal skins.

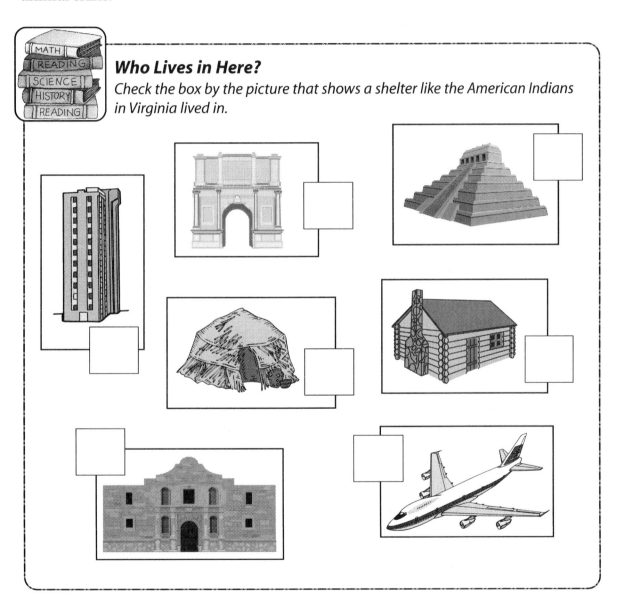

Who Lives in Here?

Check the box by the picture that shows a shelter like the American Indians in Virginia lived in.

CLOTHING

American Indians in Virginia made clothing from animal skins (deerskin).

The climate experienced by American Indians is much the same as it is today. Virginia's climate varies by location based on two things:

What Should I Wear?

Check the box by the picture that shows what American Indians in Virginia used for making clothes.

~ This book is not reproducible. ~

Background Check!

Pretend you are a member of the Powhatan tribe at the time of the first European explorers. You were perfectly happy farming, hunting, and fishing. What do you think of their:

*Food?*_____

*Clothing?*_____

*Shelters?*_____

• **Elevation:** The mountains in western Virginia experience cooler weather because or their high elevation.
• **Distance from the ocean:** The plains and coastal area have warmer weather because of warm air currents from the ocean.

Essential Skills

Write the number from the map next to the correct statement about Virginia's climate.

_____ *American Indians worked harder to stay warm in this area.*

_____ *American Indians in this area enjoyed warmer weather than other parts of the state.*

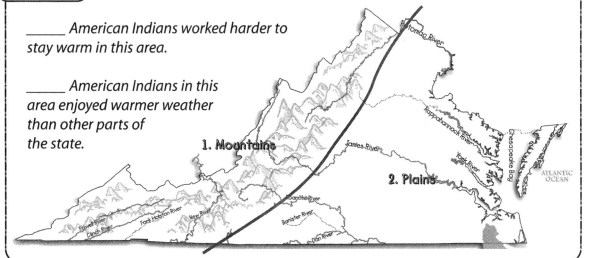

This one's ALL for fun! See if you can find the Virginia cities and landmarks in the Word Search! (Hints: the first or last letter of the city name rests NEAR the actual spot where you would find the city on a real map; other names are hidden both on and off the map. So, if you know your geography, this will take no time at all!)

Alexandria
Appalachian Plateau
Appomattox
Blue Ridge Mountains
Bristol
Charlottesville
Chesapeake Bay
Danville

Emporia
Fall Line
Fredericksburg
Harrisonburg
James River
Jamestown
Leesburg
Lexington

Lynchburg
Richmond
Monticello
Mount Rogers
Mount Vernon
Norfolk
Piedmont
Potomac

Roanoke
Shenandoah
Tidewater
Valley and Ridge
Waynesboro
Williamsburg
Winchester

```
V V P I E D M O N T D J S V S M C J S D Y S K F K B M X M S G P W R I G V N
A S A B S G M R U I J F J D D S W I N C H E S T E R E O F J F O I L J V H C
L H S F H E O A N D O A H E J I H W O I L E E S B U R G E S T L R A K X H
L N D A G H U S H E N A N D O A H F T R H A L E X A N D R I A O L I M G T E
E D D L S A N A L W V J V L A S D G V B M O U N T V E R N O N M I K E O H S
Y K S L E K T K N A S H A R R I S O N B U R G W J V K S D E G A A G S S J A
A I A L V B R S H T J B M F J S F R E D E R I C K S B U R G D C M V R R K P
N S K I B L O D K E G W A Y N E S B O R O C C C H A R L O T T E S V I L L E
D D J N Y S G E U R J L E X I N G T O N G I M O N T I C E L L O B D V G H A
R L L E G H E N Y A P P A L A C H I A N P L A T E A U I D T T V U D E D K K
I Q Q W J B R H X F D M N H J F Y T B H R I C H M O N D F G A R S R K K E
D H F G Y T S J I O F L Y N C H B U R G Y A P P O M A T T O X E F G V B C F B
G O O H P R I U D R O A N O K E F O F A S D E J A M E S T O W N F G M M A
E D F Y K H G J B L U E R I D G E M O U N T A I N S G T N O R F O L K G U Y
J B R I S T O L B K V L D A N V I L L E S J E M P O R I A U R E P O I L F H
```

A Quick Review For You!

Circle the letter of the correct answers.

1. Which is NOT one of Virginia's regions?
    A. Coastal Plain (Tidewater)
    B. Piedmont
    C. Grand Canyon
    D. Blue Ridge Mountains

2. Which state borders Virginia?
    A. Texas
    B. Tennessee
    C. Michigan
    D. Georgia

3. Which water feature was important to the development of Virginia?
    A. Chesapeake Bay
    B. Baffin Bay
    C. Bay of Bengal
    D. Hudson Bay

4. Who were the first people to live in Virginia?
    A. Settlers at Jamestown
    B. American Indians
    C. English
    D. Spanish

5. What covers most of Virginia's land?
    A. Dry desert
    B. Glaciers
    C. Tundra
    D. Forests

A Quick Review For You!
Circle the letter of the correct answers.

6. How did American Indians adapt to their environment?
    A. Hunted food and picked berries
    B. Made clothing from animal skins
    C. Built shelters from natural materials
    D. All of these

7. What is the climate in Virginia like?
    A. Always hot
    B. Four seasons
    C. Always cold
    D. None of these

8. Why did Christopher Columbus call the people he found "Indians"?
    A. He thought he was in the Indies (near China)
    B. He thought he was in India
    C. It was carved on a tree
    D. The King told him to call them Indians

9. Which River flows into the Chesapeake River?
    A. James River
    B. York River
    C. Potomac River
    D. All of these

10. What is a peninsula?
    A. An island with no bridge to it
    B. A crater with water in it
    C. A narrow piece of land with water on three sides
    D. A swamp with crocodiles

Section 2

Colonization and Conflict: 1607 Through the American Revolution

The Virginia colonists brought very little with them to the New World. This is one reason they had such a difficult time getting settled in Jamestown. However, they were influenced by their former lives in England as they began to establish their own culture and society in this new, raw land.

Chapter 2

VS.3a — The English wanted to colonize America for several reasons.
Correlates with VS.1c, VS.1d, VS.1g, and VS.1i.

The Virginia Company of London and the Virginia Colony

Some European countries, including England, were in competition to increase their wealth and power by expanding their empires to America. England wanted to establish an American colony to increase her wealth and power. England hoped to find silver and gold in America. England knew that an American settlement would furnish raw materials that could not be grown or obtained in England. A new colony would also open new markets for trade.

colony: a group of people who settle in a distant territory but remain subject to (ruled by) their parent country

The stockholders of the Virginia Company of London financed the settlement of Jamestown. Jamestown was primarily an economic venture; stockholders wanted to make money. Jamestown became the first permanent English settlement in North America in 1607.

Check which came first:

___The Virginia colony   ___The Virginia Company of London

If you participate in an economic venture, you hope to:

___A. Make money
___B. Lose money

economics: the science that deals with the production, distribution, and consumption of goods and services

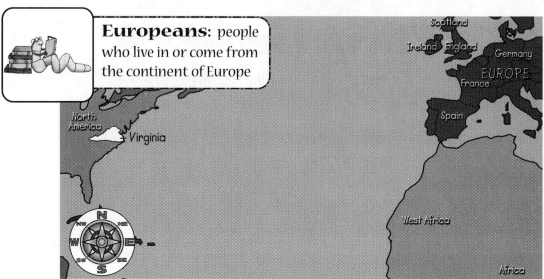

Europeans: people who live in or come from the continent of Europe

 Draw a dashed (— — —) line from the coast of England to the coast of Virginia.

Economic Interdependence

The Virginia colony and England were economically interdependent. England depended on raw materials exported from the Virginia colony. The Virginia colony depended on imported manufactured goods from England.

1. An example of economic interdependence is:
___A. You are independently wealthy.
___B. You trade vegetables that you have grown in your garden for some homemade bread from a neighbor.

Raw materials exported from the Virginia colony to England included wood used for shipbuilding. Manufactured goods imported from England to the Virginia colony included clothing, iron pots, and tools.

2. Raw materials are:
___A. uncooked
___B. clothing
___C. things used to make a final product

3. Manufactured goods are:
___A. made from raw materials
___B. found in the earth

Here Come the Europeans!

When settlers arrived in 1607, Jamestown was located on a narrow peninsula bordered on three sides by the James River. Today, Jamestown is located on an island in the James River.

English: people who live in or come from the country of England

The English settled in Jamestown at the mouth of the James River for three very good reasons:

- The location was easy to defend (in case they were attacked by the Spanish Navy).
- The water along the shore was deep enough for ships to dock.
- They believed they had a good supply of fresh water.

Put a ● on the area where the English settled when they first came to Virginia.

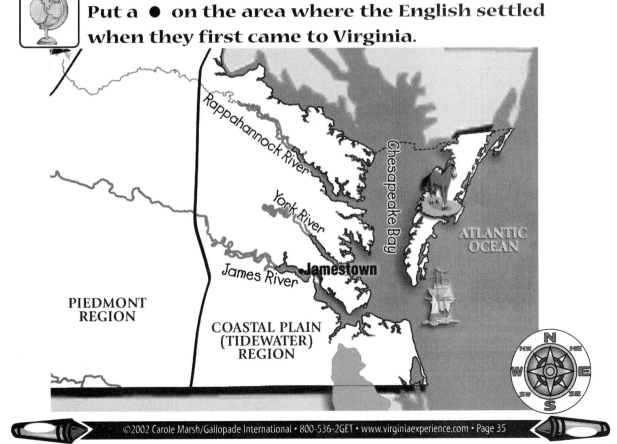

Background check

Jamestown became the first permanent English colony in America. The Virginia Company investors hoped to make a quick profit from gold or other valuables. The first colonists, 104 men and boys, came to Jamestown for other reasons. Some of them hoped to get rich, and some were excited about the adventure. (A few them were probably scared, too). The colonists hoped to explore Virginia and trade with American Indians. Many members of the original group of colonists died of disease or starvation. More colonists came in 1608 and 1609. So many of them died during the winter of 1609–1610 that this period became known as "the starving time."

Great Debate

It's been a rough start in the new settlement at Jamestown. How would you feel if you were a…

1. Stockholder in the Virginia Company

_____

_____

2. Very sick colonist

_____

_____

3. Colonist who was healthy

_____

_____

4. Mother of one of the boys who went to Jamestown

_____

_____

5. American Indian who traded with the colonists

_____

_____

VS.3c—The Charters of the Virginia Company of London were important in establishing the Jamestown settlement. Correlates with VS.1a, VS.1d, VS.1e, VS.1f, and VS.1g.

They Chartered Themselves a Colony!

The King of England granted charters to the Virginia Company of London.

The charters gave the Virginia Company the right to establish a settlement in North America.

charter: a document issued by a government authority

The charters extended English rights to the colonists.

The first charter of the Virginia Company of London established companies to begin colonies in the New World.

List three effects of charters allowing settlements in North America.

1. _____

2. _____

3. _____

Question for Discussion
How is American life today affected by the decision to allow a North American establishment?

English Law Rules!

England and the Virginia colony had an economic relationship and a political relationship. The Virginia colony, though far away from its parent country, was subject to (had to obey) English law.

politics: the activities related to a government

Pretend that you have left your country and moved across a large body of water to a new place. The leaders in your country want to continue to tell you what to do, even though they are not there to see what your life is like. What might you tell the leaders where you're from?

_____

_____

_____

Now pretend that you are the king and no one will do what they are told. Write a letter to your disobedient subjects.

_____

_____

_____

Diary Discovery

Pretend you are reading a diary entry written by a Jamestown settler.

I spent all day searching for gold. I didn't find any. Tomorrow, I shall try to get some food from the Indians. If they won't give me any more, maybe I can steal some from one of the other colonists. There aren't any inns that serve a hot meal, or any farmers, or any butcher shops here in the Virginia colony. It's hard to find a good meal here.

Why was it hard to get a "good meal" in the Virginia colony?

_____

Virginia Establishes Its Own Government

Although people in the Virginia colony did not always like being subject to the laws of a faraway country, they respected the system of government that they had always known. As Jamestown grew, the system of government evolved.

In 1619, the governor of Virginia called a meeting of the Virginia Assembly. The Assembly included two citizen representatives (called "burgesses") from each of the divisions of Virginia, the governor's council, and the governor. (At that time, only adult men were considered citizens.) By the 1640s, the burgesses became a separate legislative body, called the Virginia House of Burgesses.

Virginia House of Burgesses

- It was the first elected legislative body in America. It gave settlers the opportunity to control their own government.
- It became the General Assembly. It is the oldest legislative body in the Western Hemisphere.

1. How did early Virginians show respect for the English form of government?

___A. They ignored it.

___B. They copied certain ideas and systems in their new government.

Write E if the phrase describes England.
Write A if the phrase describes America.
Write B if the phrase describes both England and America.

_____ **2.** Economically interdependent

_____ **3.** Voters elect representatives

_____ **4.** Imported manufactured goods

_____ **5.** Founded colonies across the ocean

_____ **6.** Subject to laws from parent country

Background Check

The House of Burgesses first met at Jamestown on July 30, 1619. Governor Sir George Yeardley called the meeting. The session included two burgesses from each of the 11 boroughs of Virginia. Their first act was to approve an official great seal for the colony. Seals are often used on official and important documents to prove that they are trustworthy.

Virginia's Current State Seal

Question for discussion

Why do you think the House of Burgesses' first order of business was to approve an official great seal for the Virginia colony?

burgess: citizen of a borough

A Quick Review for You!

Number these events in the order that they happened.

THEN

☐ THE FIRST MEETING OF THE HOUSE OF BURGESSES

☐ ENGLISH COLONISTS ESTABLISH JAMESTOWN

☐ VIRGINIA HOUSE OF BURGESSES APPROVES OFFICIAL SEAL

☐ POWHATAN TRIBE LIVES IN VIRGINIA

NOW

Help is On the Way!

Jamestown became a more diverse colony by 1620. The arrival of women in 1620 made it possible for the settlers to establish families and a more permanent settlement at Jamestown. Women did chores and educated the children. The first English women came to the Jamestown colony as "mail order brides." These brides had a price! A settler had to pay 120 pounds (54 kilograms) of tobacco, the price of a woman's ship passage, to gain the right to say, "I do."

The first women in Jamestown probably worried that no one would pay for their journey. They faced an uncertain future in a new unexplored wilderness. How would you have felt if you had been one of these women?

_____

_____

_____

Tobacco in Colonial Virginia

In 1612, Virginia colonist John Rolfe experimented with growing tobacco. Two years later, he learned how to "cure" the green leaves until they were brown. He shipped these dried leaves back to England, where people in fashionable society learned (cough! cough!) to enjoy smoking.

Hard-To-Believe-But-True!

The success of tobacco as a money-making crop was astounding. From four barrels shipped in 1614, the quantity grew to 2,500 pounds (1,125 kilograms), then 50,000 pounds (22,500 kilograms), and by 1628, 500,000 pounds (225,000 kilograms)! In addition to making money for the colony, tobacco itself was used as money.

Africans Arrive in Virginia

As plantations in the Tidewater region expanded, more hands were needed to work the land. People were needed to plant, grow, and harvest the crops. Africans were brought to Virginia as a source of labor. They were brought by ship from Africa. Africans arrived in Jamestown against their will.

The first group of Africans arrived in Jamestown in 1619. It is believed that Africans arrived as baptized Christians; therefore, they were considered indentured servants for a period of 5 to 7 years.

The arrival of Africans made it possible to expand the tobacco economy.

 Draw a dashed (– – – –) line from Africa to Virginia.

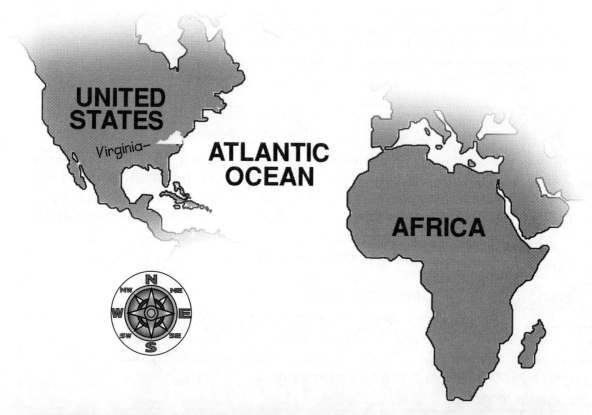

Tobacco dominated Virginia's colonial economy because:

- Virginia had plenty of farmland on which to grow it.
- The arrival of Africans provided labor to grow it.
- England and the rest of Europe were willing to pay a lot of money for tobacco.
- People raising tobacco made high profits.

The tobacco introduced by John Rolfe became the foundation of colonial Virginia's economy. The Virginia soil and climate are excellent for growing tobacco. Tobacco is still an important crop in Virginia and other parts of the South.

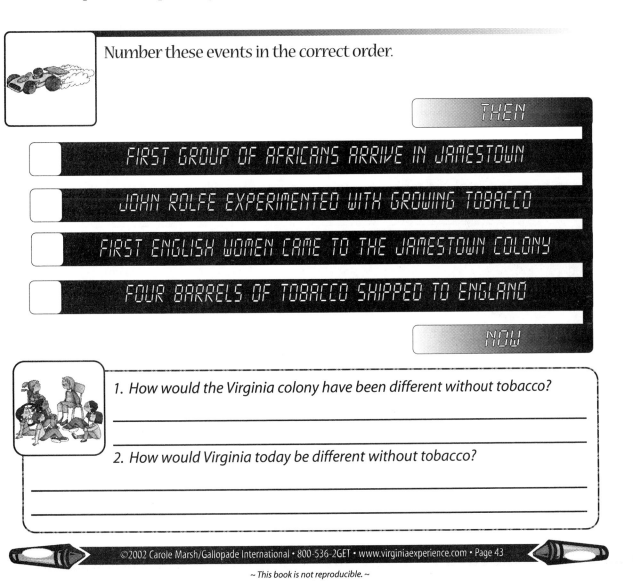

Number these events in the correct order.

THEN

FIRST GROUP OF AFRICANS ARRIVE IN JAMESTOWN

JOHN ROLFE EXPERIMENTED WITH GROWING TOBACCO

FIRST ENGLISH WOMEN CAME TO THE JAMESTOWN COLONY

FOUR BARRELS OF TOBACCO SHIPPED TO ENGLAND

NOW

1. How would the Virginia colony have been different without tobacco?

_____

_____

2. How would Virginia today be different without tobacco?

_____

_____

VS.3f—Settlers at Jamestown were faced with hardships and forced to make changes in order to ensure their survival. Correlates with VS.1b, VS.1c, VS.1d, VS.1f, and VS.1g.

Survival of the Fittest

The English colonists found life in Jamestown more difficult than they had expected. The colonists brought very little with them to the New World. The settlers at Jamestown faced many hardships.

Help Wanted: Strong, brave men needed to take part in the Virginia Experience. See the beauty of nature! Meet friendly natives! Find adventure and gold on a distant shore!

- The site they chose to live on was marshy, and the drinking water was impure and unsafe to drink.

- The settlers lacked some skills necessary to provide for themselves. The first settlers at Jamestown came to America mostly to search for treasure. Few of the men were able or willing to do manual labor or farm.

- Many settlers died of starvation and disease. An unwholesome diet weakened the men. About two-thirds of them soon died of malnutrition, malaria, pneumonia, and dysentery. Sharp sudden changes in weather added to their problems.

Circle the things settlers in Virginia would need.

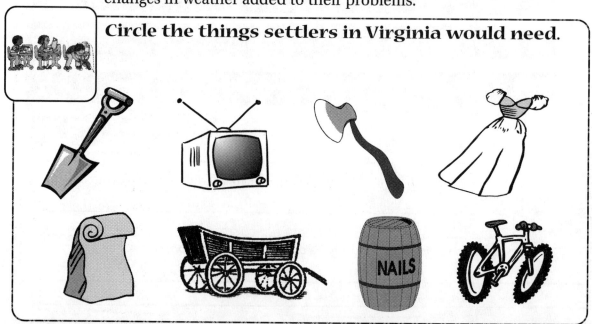

Time for a Change!

Survival of the settlement at Jamestown was ensured by these changes:
- Arrival of two supply ships
- Forced work program
- Strong leadership of Captain John Smith
- Emphasis on self-sustaining agriculture

From the Journals of Captain John Smith, mid-1608 to mid-1609...

...I have had to force the adventuresome colonists to abandon their fruitless treasure hunting and get to work preparing the Jamestown settlement for the coming winter. We will all surely freeze or starve to death if the men do not start working for their survival. I have decreed:

He Who Will Not Work, Shall Not Eat!

...I have befriended the local people, the Powhatans. As I am the leader of the council of the colonists' advisors. I believe that these natives consider me to be a "white chief." The Powhatan have offered their help. They are showing us how to plant various crops, and they are teaching us how to hunt.

...My men have been productive over the past few months! They planted corn at the end of spring and are learning to hunt for food. They have built a number of shelters that will keep us warm through the winter, and they are building more. We are also building a fort from which can defend our growing settlement...

...The Jamestown settlement is thriving! I regret that this will be the last entry I write while in our colony. My leg has been injured in a gunpowder explosion. I am returning to England for treatment. Perhaps, once I have recovered from this injury, I will return to Jamestown.

captain john smith

Captain John Smith provided much needed leadership to the first colonists at Jamestown. His biggest contribution was creating rules which the colonists lived by. The most famous of these was, "He Who Will Not Work, Shall Not Eat!"

After leaving, Captain John Smith never revisited Jamestown. He lived there for only 18 months, but made a world of difference!

JOHN SMITH RULES!

Once the colonists landed at Jamestown, Captain John Smith realized they needed rules to survive. **Rule 1: You had to work to eat!**
How was life different after the arrival of Captain John Smith?

_____

_____

How do rules make life better today?

_____

_____

A Quick Review For You!

1. Which came first?

____ Captain John Smith arrived in the Virginia colony.

____ Colonists founded Jamestown.

2. The Virginia colonists survived because they…

A. Looked for gold

B. Planted crops for food

C. Did not work

3. Captain John Smith made life better for the Virginia colony.

A. True   B. False

4. How do you think Virginians felt when John Smith said, "He who will not work, shall not eat"?

_____

_____

A Quick Review for You!

1. What caused Jamestown settlers to die?
    a. Starvation
    b. Diseases
    c. Both of the above

2. What hardships did the Jamestown settlers face?
    a. Marshy land
    b. Impure drinking water
    c. Lack of farming skills
    d. All of the above

3. What changes took place that ensured the settlers' survival?
    a. Supply ships
    b. Forced work programs
    c. Leadership of Captain John Smith
    d. All of the above

Which happened first? Number the items in each pair in order.

_____ Smith hurt his leg in a gunpowder explosion.

_____ Smith was leader of the council of the colonists' advisors.

_____ The settlers at Jamestown faced many hardships.

_____ The settlers left England for the new colony.

_____ Settlers spent time searching for gold and silver.

_____ Smith forced settlers to hunt food, plant corn, and build shelters.

Progress with the Powhatan People!

Captain John Smith initiated trading relationships with the Powhatan. For a while, the Powhatan people and the English had positive interactions. The Powhatan helped the English survive in their new home. The Powhatan people traded food, furs, and leather with the English in exchange for tools, pots, guns, and other goods.

interactions: communication or activity among two or more people

 Label the English items with an "E."
Labels the Powhatan items with a "P."

The Powhatan people contributed to the survival of the Jamestown settlers in several ways:

- Pocahontas, daughter of Chief Powhatan, believed that the English and American Indians could live in peace and harmony.
- Pocahontas began a friendship with the colonists that helped them survive.
- The Powhatan introduced new crops to the English, including corn and tobacco.

Captain John Smith wrote about how Pocahontas saved his life. He wrote in his book that Chief Powhatan was about to kill him with a stone war club. Pocahontas placed her head over Smith's and begged her father to spare him. (It is not certain whether this is a true story.)

Enrichment Exercise

Number the events depicted below in chronological order (the order in which they occurred).

Captain John Smith initiated trading with the Powhatan.

Captain John Smith leaves the Virginia colony.

Powhatan people live before settlers arrive.

The English had positive interactions with the Powhatan.

Question for Discussion

How do you think the Powhatan people and the Jamestown settlers communicated?

_____

_____

In 1614, the English kidnapped Pocahontas. During this time, she and John Rolfe fell in love. Their marriage marked the beginning of a period of peace between American Indians and the Jamestown colonists.

Rolfe served as the colony's secretary from 1614 to 1619. Rolfe, Pocahontas, and their infant son, Thomas, traveled to England in 1616, to help raise funds for the struggling colonists in Virginia. In 1617, while waiting to sail back to America, Pocahontas died of smallpox.. Rolfe returned to America and later remarried.

The relationship between the Jamestown settlers and the Powhatans changed when the Powhatan people realized the English settlement would continue to grow. The Powhatans saw the colonists as invaders that would take over their land.

The Great Debate!

Pretend a settler and a Powhatan are having a debate over the land. They cannot agree with each other.
*Put an "**S**" by the **settler's** comments.*
*Put a "**P**" by the **Powhatan's** comments.*

_____ *"I was here first. Why don't you go back to where you came from?"*

_____ *"No one owns this land. I'm going to claim it for myself and build a farm on it."*

_____ *"To make the land habitable, forests and trees should be cleared, and wild animals should be killed."*

_____ *"I respect nature, the animals, and the Great Spirit."*

_____ *"Man can live in harmony with nature."*

A Quick Review For You!

Circle the letter of the correct answers.

1. What change ensured the survival of the settlement at Jamestown?
    A. Strong leadership of Captain John Smith
    B. Strong leadership of Captain Jesse James
    C. Strong leadership of Captain James Kirk
    D. No leadership (No one telling them what to do!)

2. What did Pocahontas, daughter of Chief Powhatan, believed that
    A. English colonists and American Indians would go to war
    B. English colonists and American Indians could live in peace
    C. English colonists and American Indians shouldn't speak
    D. Pocahontas never met any English colonists

3. If you participate in an economic venture, you hope to:
    A. Lose money
    B. Make money
    C. Borrow money
    D. Open a savings account

4. What are raw materials?
    A. A final product
    B. Things that are used to make a final product
    C. Furniture
    D. Clothing

5. Which one was NOT a reason the English settled at Jamestown?
    A. Location was easy to defend (from the Spanish Navy)
    B. Water along the shore was deep enough for ships to dock
    C. They believed they had a good supply of fresh water
    D. The area had a good school system

A Quick Review For You!

Circle the letter of the correct answers.

6. Which came first?
    A. Captain John Smith arrived in the Virginia colony
    B. Colonists founded Jamestown
    C. John Rolfe began growing tobacco in Jamestown
    D. Powhatan people lived in Virginia

7. What is a charter?
    A. Underside of a ship
    B. Map used to find the way to Jamestown
    C. A document issued by a government authority
    D. Special kind of tobacco

8. Which statement describes the Virginia House of Burgesses?
    A. First elected legislative body in America
    B. Became the General Assembly
    C. Oldest legislative body in the Western Hemisphere
    D. All of these

9. Why did tobacco dominate Virginia's colonial economy?
    A. Virginia had plenty of farmland on which to grow it.
    B. The arrival of Africans provided labor to grow it.
    C. People raising tobacco made high profits.
    D. All of these

10. How did the arrival of women in Jamestown change the colony?
    A. Made it possible for the settlers to establish families
    B. Made a more permanent settlement at Jamestown
    C. Both A and B
    D. None of these

Chapter 3

VS.4a—Agriculture was a major influence on the institution of slavery.
Correlates with VS.1b, VS.1d, VS.1e, and VS.1f.

Money Does Grow — On Tobacco Farms!

The economy of the Virginia colony depended on agriculture as a primary source of wealth. Tobacco became the most profitable agricultural product.

cash crop: a crop that is grown to sell for money rather than for use by the growers

Tobacco was sold in England as a cash crop. Tobacco saved the Virginia colony, as it gave the people a way to support themselves. By the time John Rolfe introduced it to the Virginia colony, Europeans were already familiar with tobacco. Christopher Columbus brought some tobacco seeds back to Europe where farmers began growing the plant for use as a medicine.

!?!

Today, farmers grow tobacco on only a small part of Virginia's cropland, but tobacco makes more money than any other crop. Tobacco products rank second among goods manufactured in Virginia.

```
A H N R C X T S B C E E L
R P L T O B A C C O C P E
U E G O R R R U H R G O E
T A X M A N P T A N T T K
A N O A P P L E S W F A S
B U T T E R R W Q I V T L
A T N O R B L X U J M O M
G S N E R J H A Y W K E E
A L M S O Y B E A N S S T
```

Find these Virginia crops in the word search below!

corn
hay
tobacco
soybeans
apples
tomatoes
potatoes
peanuts

Agriculture in the Virginia colony encouraged the institution of slavery. The successful planting of tobacco depended on a reliable and inexpensive source of labor. Large numbers of Africans were brought to the colony against their will to work as slaves on the plantations. The Virginia colony became dependent on slave labor, and the dependence lasted a long time. The success of tobacco as a cash crop transformed life in the Virginia colony and encouraged slavery.

Background Check!

Raising tobacco is no easy job. Seeds are planted in a seed bed and must be covered with a cloth for 8–12 weeks. Then the plants are replanted in a field, where the soil is repeatedly cultivated. When the plants start to produce flowers, the upper part of the plants are topped (cut off), making the leaves grow bigger.

When the harvest comes, the leaves are picked or the whole stalk is cut. The plants are placed on sticks and left in the field for a couple of days so they will wilt. The tobacco must then be cured in large barns built just for curing tobacco. Curing can take anywhere from a few days to several weeks.

That's a LOT of work!

What effect did agriculture have on the Virginia colony?

_____

How did agriculture in the Virginia colony influence the institution of slavery?

_____

Which came first?

_____ A. Tobacco in the Virginia colony

_____ B. Slavery in the Virginia colony

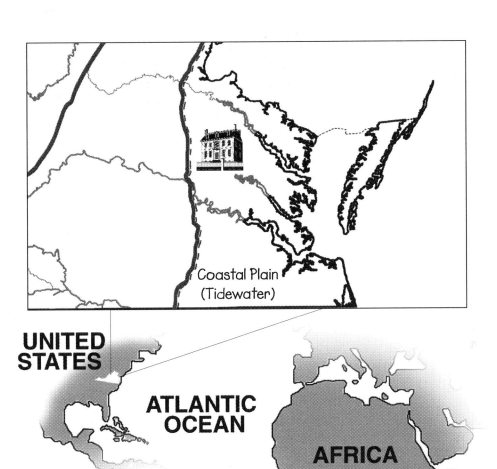

Coastal Plain
(Tidewater)

UNITED
STATES

ATLANTIC
OCEAN

AFRICA

Locate Africa on the map. ....Write an "S" for slaves.

Locate the Tidewater region of Virginia. ....Write an "L" for labor.

Locate the Atlantic Ocean. ....Write an "A" for the Atlantic.

Locate Virginia on the map. ....Write a "V" for Virginia.

Locate a plantation in the Tidewater region. ......Write an "E" for expansion.

VS.4b—Immigrants including Europeans (English, Scotch-Irish, and German), and Africans and American Indians influenced the cultural landscape and changed the relationship between the Virginia colony and England. Correlates with VS.1b, VS.1c, VS.1d, VS.1g, and VS.1i.

Culture Shock!

Whenever people settle an area, they change the landscape to reflect the beliefs, customs, and architecture of their culture. Examples of cultural landscapes include:

culture: shared beliefs or values of a group

- Buildings (barns, homes, commercial and industrial places)
- Places of worship
- Landscaping (style of arranging trees, walkways, gardens and buildings)

Essential Skills

Circle the examples of cultural landscapes.

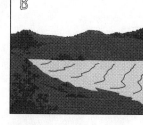

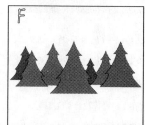

Everyone Contributes!

Many different groups of people made important contributions to the development of the Virginia colony.

The different groups of people who contributed to the success of the Virginia colony included the American Indians, the English, the Germans, Scotch-Irish, and the African slaves.

contribute: to help, to take part in, to do your share

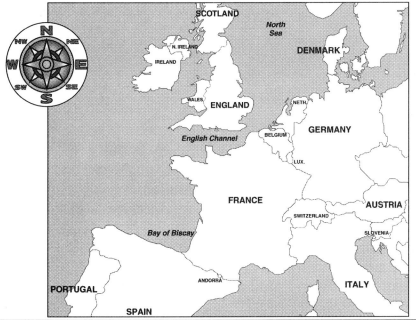

Where did people in colonial Virginia come from? The American Indians were already living on the land.

Using the map above, complete this Quick Quiz:

1. Circle the countries that sent settlers to Virginia.

2. Underline the name of the country whose settlers landed in Jamestown first.

3. Find the ocean European settlers had to cross to get to America. Write its name in the correct area.

Here is a map showing where the different cultural groups settled. Migration and living in new areas caused people to adapt old customs to their new environment.

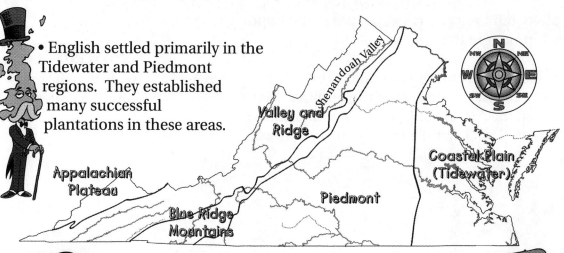

• English settled primarily in the Tidewater and Piedmont regions. They established many successful plantations in these areas.

Shenandoah Valley

Valley and Ridge

Coastal Plain (Tidewater)

Appalachian Plateau

Piedmont

Blue Ridge Mountains

• Germans and Scotch-Irish settled primarily in the Shenandoah Valley, which was along the migration route to unsettled territory. They hoped to establish new settlements.

• American Indians (First Americans) were primarily in the Tidewater, Piedmont, and Appalachian Plateau regions, where their traditional homelands and hunting grounds were located.

• Africans settled (against their will) primarily in the Tidewater and Piedmont regions, where agriculture required a great deal of labor.

migrate: to move from one region or country to another

Question for Discussion
Think about the reasons that Africans and American Indians settled where they did. How are the reasons similar? How are they different?

On the timeline below, number the order in which these major events occurred in early Virginia history.

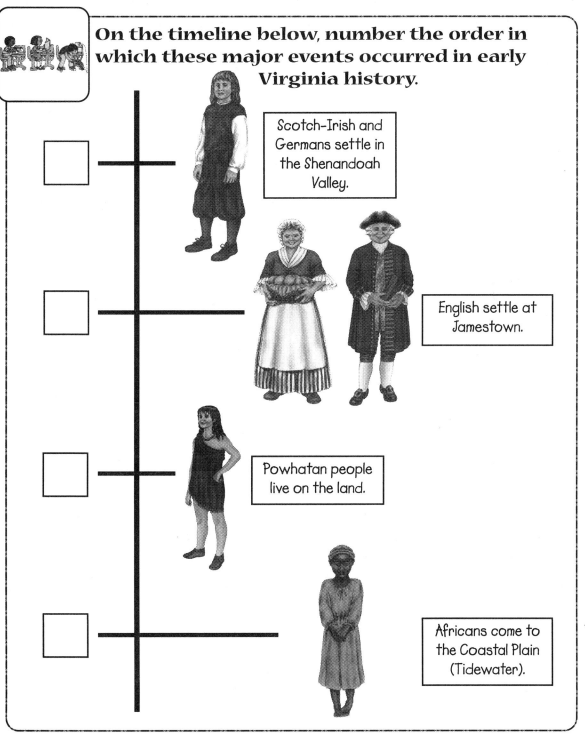

Scotch-Irish and Germans settle in the Shenandoah Valley.

English settle at Jamestown.

Powhatan people live on the land.

Africans come to the Coastal Plain (Tidewater).

Map Skills!

Analyze the map to answer the following questions.

Label the map with the five regions. Then label the Shenandoah Valley.

1. Which area(s) did the Germans and Scotch-Irish settle? Write **G+S-I** in the area(s).

2. Which area(s) did the English settle? Write **E** in the area(s).

3. Which area(s) did the Africans settle? Write **Af** in the area(s).

4. Which area(s) did the American Indians (First Americans) live in before the arrival of other immigrants? Write **Am** in the area(s).

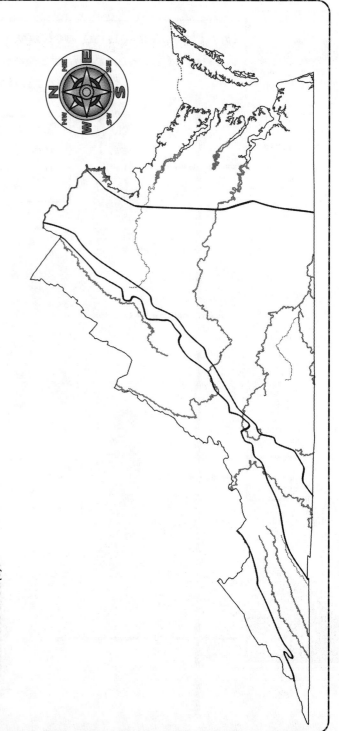

Making a Contribution!

American Indians taught colonists survival strategies.

strategy: a plan of action; a way to get things done

Match the skill taught with the result.

1. How to grow crops   2. How to store crops through the winter   3. How to hunt game

A. They had meat to eat.   B. They harvested food to eat.   C. They did not starve.

Match the colonial Virginia person below with the letter of the diary entry that they might have made.

1 - slave ____

2 - Virginia Company of London member ____

3 - indentured servant ____

4 - House of Burgesses member ____

5 - plantation owner ____

6 - German/Scotch-Irish farmer ____

7 - mother ____

A - "Another day working to pay off my debt has gone by."

B - "It was a very hot day to pick tobacco!"

C - "The children made good progress in their studies today."

D - "The clouds that came over the Blue Ridge mountains brought rain to our crops today."

E - "I hope there will be enough tobacco for our company to make a profit this year."

F - "No matter how many people I have working on the land, I always seem to need more!"

G - "I think we did a good job representing the people today."

Although a colony of England, Virginia developed a unique culture different from that of England. The culture of Virginia reflected American Indian (First American), African, and European origins. Migration and living in new areas caused people to adapt old customs to their new environment.

Place names reflect culture:
• English — Richmond, Newport News, Norfolk
• American Indian — Roanoke, Chesapeake, Potomac

Enriching Map Skill Exercise!

Which culture named the cities on the map below? Fill in the table with some of the city names.

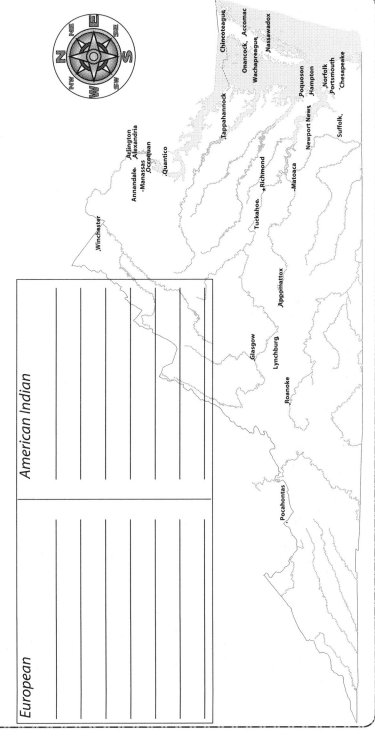

European	American Indian

~ This book is not reproducible. ~

Location, Location, Location!

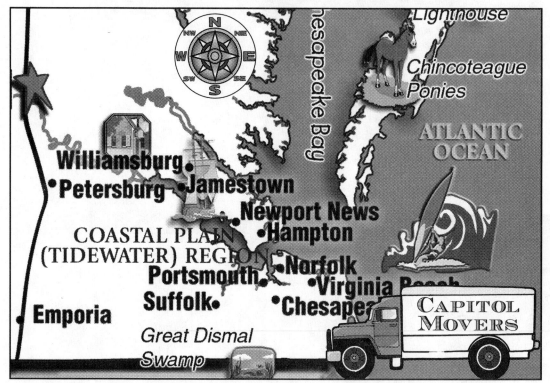

Swampland Makes a Good Home . . . for Crocodiles!

Geographical factors often influence the location of a capital. Here are some factors that influenced moving the colonial capital from Jamestown to Williamsburg in 1699.

- Drinking water was contaminated by seepage of salt water
- Dirty living conditions caused diseases
- Williamsburg was situated at a higher elevation than Jamestown
- Fire destroyed wooden buildings at Jamestown

Which one was NOT a cause for moving the capital from Jamestown?

_____ A. Drinking water contaminated by seepage of salt water

_____ B. Dirty living conditions caused diseases

_____ C. Loud neighbors

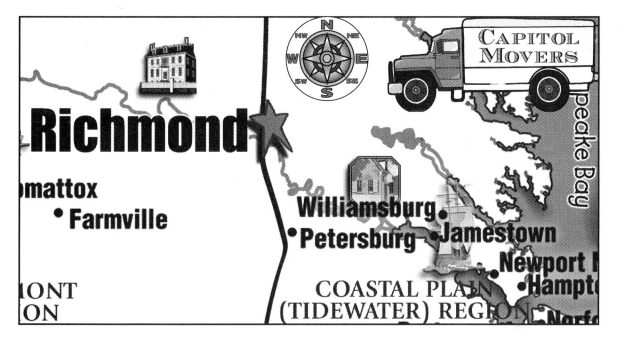

Follow that Horse-drawn Cart!!

Today, Richmond is the capital of Virginia. Some factors related to moving the colonial capital from Williamsburg to Richmond in 1780 include:
- Population was moving westward
- Richmond was a more central location
- Richmond's location was better for trade
- Moving to Richmond increased the distance from attack by the English

Number the cities in the order they became the capital of Virginia. Circle Virginia's present capital.

_____ A. Williamsburg

_____ B. Richmond

_____ C. Jamestown

How was the move to Richmond different than the move to Wiliamsburg? How were they similar?

Why Move?

Settlers who first came to Virginia settled along the coast. Soon, they began to move inland to other parts of the state.

What causes people to move from one location to another? Here are just a few reasons:

Necessity: *They may need more space to grow crops.*

Preference: *Perhaps they prefer a cooler climate, a city over the countryside, or to be closer to their work, other family members, or new opportunities.*

Curiosity: *Some people want to try new places, to see different areas.*

Opportunity: *They may even believe that there are better opportunities in other geographic locations than where they currently live and work.*

How many times have you moved so far in your lifetime? _____

How many states have you lived in? _____
Name them:

_____

_____

_____

How many towns/cities have you lived in? _____
Name them:

_____

_____

_____

VS.4d — Money, barter, and credit were used in the Virginia colony. Correlates with VS.1b, VS.1c, VS.1d, VS.1e, VS.1f, and VS.1i.

Money was not commonly used in early agricultural societies. Colonial Virginia had no banks. Few people had paper money and coins to use to buy goods and services. *Barter* was commonly used instead of money.

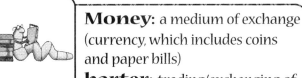

Money: a medium of exchange (currency, which includes coins and paper bills)
barter: trading/exchanging of goods and services without the use of money

Barter was commonly used among the colonists to obtain the things that they needed or wanted. To barter is to trade or swap one thing for another without using money. For example, a colonist who had extra corn might trade it for some fresh eggs from a colonist who owned a hen. Tobacco was a highly valued barter item. It was often used instead of money. A tobacco farmer could use his tobacco to pay for goods and services.

Essential Bartering Skills

Circle the items below which might serve as something with which you could barter.

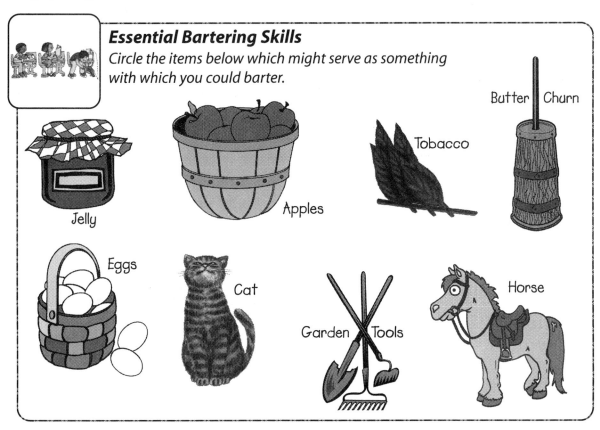

Jelly

Apples

Tobacco

Butter Churn

Eggs

Cat

Garden Tools

Horse

Essential Bartering Skills, Part Two
*Circle the **colonial services** for which you might barter some of the goods previously pictured.*

Pottery

Dental work

Tow your car

Lawn service

A haircut

Blacksmithing

Carpentry

1. How are barter and money similar?

_____

_____

_____

2. How are they different?

_____

_____

_____

_____

Essential Bartering Skills, Part 3

It has been a busy morning on the farm. Your father is busy repairing tools. Your mother is busy preparing dinner. They send you to barter with merchants and shopkeepers for some things that they need. They give you a basket of fresh vegetables, a handmade blanket, and a fresh-baked pie. They also give you a list of items that they need: a pair of shoes for your little brother, some cornmeal, and nails.

Match the item that you would barter with the good that you receive in exchange.

Barter one
of these:

For one
of these:

Your Credit is Good Here

Farmers and other consumers could also buy goods and services on credit and pay their debts when their crops were harvested and sold.

debt: a good or service owed to another

credit: receiving a good or service now and paying for it later

saving: money put away to save or to spend at a later time

Between barter and credit, the colonists managed to survive economically without actually having very much money. Today, we do not barter as much as colonists did. We pay cash for items we want or need. Or, we put our money in banks and write checks and use debit cards for goods and services. We may use credit cards to buy on credit. We may borrow money from a bank and go into debt. And we may put our money in the bank in order to save for what we want to purchase later.

Everyone Was Part of the Economy!

Many types of people lived in the colony of Virginia. Some were wealthy plantation owners. These families enjoyed lives of luxury. However, everyone was expected to make some contribution. Even the aristocratic women spent hours doing fancy needlework. Young girls were taught these finer arts and crafts. Young boys learned plantation management at their father's side. Some of these fortunate people were the ones who established the first towns, colleges, churches, and other social institutions that helped the colony grow stronger. Some even established banks later in Virginia's history.

Other kinds of workers made their contribution to the needs of a growing society. While plantation owners generally grew tobacco, other farmers grew food crops such as wheat and corn. Artisans brought their skills with them to the colony and handcrafted fine silver or pewter dishes, tankards, and silverware. Skilled craftspeople made clothing, hats, shoes, saddles, and other goods people wanted or needed for daily life.

Other workers, such as ministers and doctors, provided services that the colonists wanted and needed. Some people ran inns or taverns; others opened shops. Less-skilled workers did menial, but necessary, work such as cleaning and hauling. No matter what their economic level, most of these colonists hoped to make more money so that they could improve the lives of their families.

Indentured servants and slaves worked hard at their jobs in the fields. However, they did not have the same motivation as those who were rewarded for hard work. Their goal was to work off their debt, or, in the case of slaves, just to survive until, perhaps, some turn of fate would offer them an opportunity for freedom.

1. Which do you think was most convenient in colonial Virginia?:
    __Credit __Barter

2. Which do you think is most convenient today?:
    __Barter __Credit

3. Which came first?
    __Money __Barter

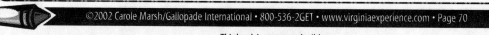

A Quick Review for YOU!

1. Few people in colonial Virginia used _____ to buy goods and services.

2. Instead of money, people would _____ with one another.

3. A valuable barter item was _____.

4. Colonists bought goods from shops on _____.

5. They would pay their _____ when the crops came in.

6. Colonists ❏ imported ❏ exported natural resources.

7. Colonists ❏ imported ❏ exported manufactured goods.

8. There were many banks in colonial Virginia. ❏ True or ❏ False?

And One More for Fun!

*You see a hoop-and-stick toy in the shop window. You **really** want it. You do not have any money. However, it is only two weeks before your farm's corn is harvested.*

Below, write what you will say to the shopkeeper to try to convince him to let you have the toy on credit.

_____

_____

_____

Chapter 4

VS.5a — The reasons the colonists went to war with England were expressed in the Declaration of Independence. Correlates with VS.1a, VS.1b, VS.1c, VS.1d, VS.1f, and VS.1g.

Conflicts developed between the colonies and England over how the colonies should be governed. The colonists and the English Parliament disagreed over this issue.

- *Parliament believed it had legal authority in the colonies, while the colonists believed their local assemblies had legal authority.*
- *Parliament believed it had the right to tax the colonies, while the colonists believed they should not be taxed since they had no representation in Parliament.*

Select the correct answer for each question.

1. Taxes are money paid:

___ A. by a government

___ B. to a government

2. Because colonists and the English could not agree:

___ A. The colonists went home to England.

___ B. The colonists wanted to make their own laws.

Discuss these conflicts in class with your classmates and teacher.

If you had a conflict with a next door neighbor, write how you might handle it.

_____

If you had a conflict with a person who lived 2,000 miles away from you, write how you might try to handle the situation.

_____

Talk about similarities and differences between conflict with English Parliament and conflict with American Indians.

A Long List of Complaints

As Virginia and the other colonies continued to grow and prosper, conflicts developed between the colonies and Great Britain (England, Scotland, and Wales). They disagreed over many things.

• The colonists and Great Britain disagreed over how to finance the French and Indian War.

• Conflict developed over the source of political authority. The colonists favored local assemblies as opposed to rule by Parliament.

• The colonists objected to taxation by England without representation.

The Declaration of Independence, written by Thomas Jefferson, states that the authority to govern belongs to the people rather than to kings. It states that all people are created equal and have rights to life, liberty, and the pursuit of happiness.

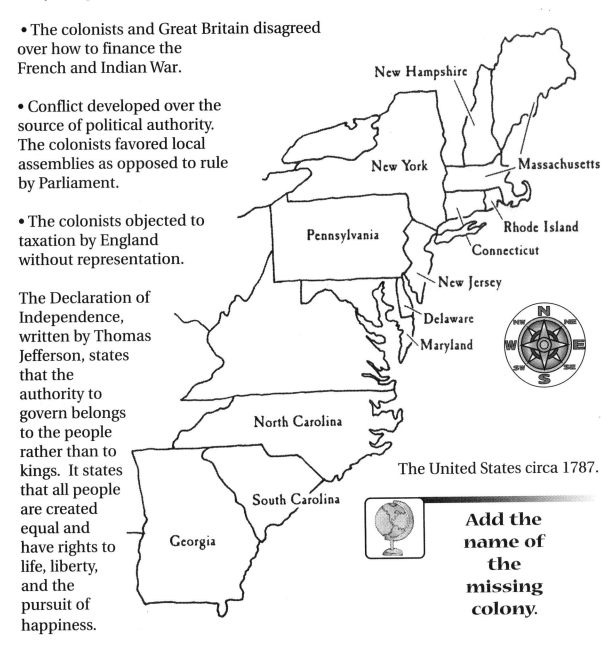

The United States circa 1787.

Add the name of the missing colony.

Conflict Was Bound to Happen

There were many conflicts between the colonies and Great Britain. Conflicts between the colonies and Great Britain eventually led the colonists to fight for freedom from their mother country. This war for independence is known as the American Revolution.

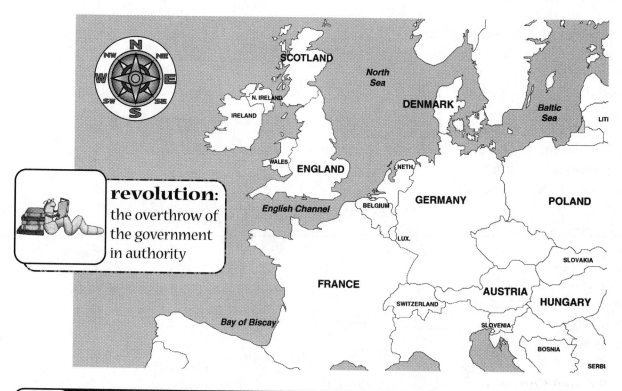

revolution: the overthrow of the government in authority

On the map above, circle the names of the places that make up Great Britain.

Which one was a country first?
_____ **United States**
_____ **Great Britain**

Let's Take a Poll!

Pretend you are a colonist.
You are asked your opinion about the following matters. Put a checkmark to indicate how you feel.

Hey, Colonists! Do we want to:

1. Pay tax, but have no say-so?	__YES __NO
2. Pay more than our fair share for war debt?	__YES __NO
3. Be ruled by faraway England?	__YES __NO
4. Establish local assemblies in the colonies?	__YES __NO
5. Fight for our independence?	__YES __NO

Conflict Leads to War!

Virginians played an active role in the colonies' struggle for independence. They participated in the events that led to war with England. Here are some of the ways that Virginians and other colonists responded to the growing conflict with Great Britain:

boycott: to not buy something as a way to protest

militia: an army made up of ordinary citizens

• Boycotted British goods

• Formed Committees of Correspondence

• Participated in Continental Congresses

• Joined militias

• Organized the Virginia Convention

• Appointed Thomas Jefferson to write the Declaration of Independence

All these activities helped put England on notice that the colonies would no longer go along with decisions being made for them. Virginians and other colonists made it clear that they wanted to be independent and make their own laws to live by. Participating in these events also helped to organize the colonists and to prepare them for the war that was to come.

Virginians and other colonists protested against unfair British rule and organized themselves for independence in many ways.

 **Circle the things that Virginians did to accomplish these things.**

 *The Declaration of Independence, written by Thomas Jefferson, gave reasons for independence and ideas for self-government. This important document states that authority to govern belongs to the people rather than to kings and that all people are created equal and have rights to life, liberty, and the pursuit of happiness.*

VS.5b — Virginians, including George Washington, Thomas Jefferson, and Patrick Henry, played an important role during the Revolutionary War era. Correlates with VS.1a and VS.1g.

Varied Roles of Virginians in the Revolutionary War Era!

Virginians made significant contributions during the Revolutionary War era. Virginia patriots served in the Continental Army and fought against the English at the Battle of Great Bridge and the siege of Yorktown. The English surrendered at Yorktown.

siege: an attack on a city or town by an army

- Some Virginians were neutral and did not take sides.
- Other Virginians remained loyal to England.
- Virginia provided food, clothing, and supplies for the Continental Army.
- During the war, women took on more responsibility. They took over the farming chores and supported troops in other ways.

Draw a circle around two of the places where Virginians fought during the Revolutionary War.

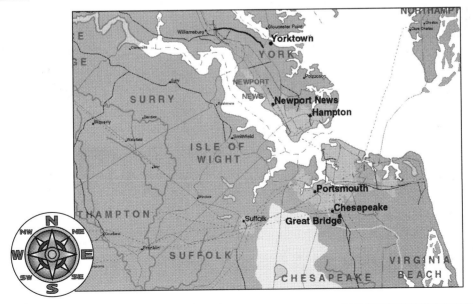

African Americans and the Revolutionary War

African Americans living in Virginia and the other colonies were divided in their feelings about the Revolutionary War. Some fought for the British because the British had promised them their freedom. Others wanted the colonists to win.

Enrichment Information

James Armistead Lafayette, a slave from Virginia, served in the Continental Army and was given his freedom after the war. He spied on the British to get information that would help the colonists win the war.

You have been a slave on a colonial plantation for many years. Now that the war with England has finally come, you must decide which side to fight for. Write your feelings here.

_____

_____

_____

_____

Number each scene to show the order in which events related to the American Revolution took place.

Pleading for representation

The battle for freedom is won

"We shall declare independence!"

At peace in the new United States

Timeline Activity:

Number these events in the order in which they happened:

☐

The Revolutionary War begins

☐

The Declaration of Independence is written

☐

Freedom! Welcome to the United States!

☐

Colonists say: "No taxation without representation!"

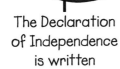

A Quick Review for YOU!

1. Virginians and other colonists did not want to pay _____ to Great Britain.

2. The colonists wanted to:
    A. Form local assemblies to govern themselves
    B. Be governed by Parliament

3. Thomas Jefferson was appointed to write the Declaration of _____.

4. During the Revolutionary War, Virginia women:
A. fought   B. farmed   C. fled

5. African Americans were _____ about the Revolutionary War.

And One More for Fun!

Match the words on the left with those on the right.

1. boycott   A. Convention

2. Committees of   B. British goods

3. Continental   C. Independence

4. Virginia   D. Correspondence

5. Declaration of   E. Congress

They Called Them the Founding Fathers for a Good Reason!

Virginia's leaders played an important role in the founding of the United States. In fact, Virginians played the largest role of all the citizens of the original colonies in the founding of the United States! Many of Virginia's first leaders were reluctant heroes. Let's take a look at some of these important Virginians.

George Washington

"I was born in Westmoreland County, Virginia, in 1732. At age 27, I became a member of the House of Burgesses. I was a delegate to the Continental Congresses in 1774 and 1775, and president of the Constitutional Convention in 1787. In 1789, I was elected — unanimously — as the first president of the United States of America. Pardon me, please, for not introducing myself. I am GEORGE WASHINGTON."

George Washington provided military leadership by serving as commander-in-chief of the Continental Army during the American Revolution. Washington was an experienced military leader and was familiar with the geography of the land.

1. The word unanimous means…
A. In anger
B. In complete agreement
C. First

Chronology of George Washington's Careers through 1775

1749 – Official surveyor for Culpeper County, Virginia

1753 – Major for the British (Delivered important communications between the governor of Virginia and French military leaders)

1754 – Colonel at Fort Necessity in the French and Indian War

1755 – Aid to British General Edward Braddock

1755-1758 – Colonel in command of Virginia's frontier troops

1774 – Delegate to First Continental Congress

1775 – Delegate to Second Continental Congress

1775 – Elected commander-in-chief by the Continental Congress

In 1775, a few days before going to Boston as commander-in-chief of the Revolutionary forces, Washington wrote:

"I am embarked on a wide ocean, boundless in its prospect and from whence, perhaps, no safe harbor is to be found."

george washington

Washington wasn't actually on the ocean, but he felt like he was trapped without a safe place to go. He agreed to become the commander-in-chief of the Continental Army. Washington was about to take on the British Empire — the most powerful military force in the world!

Question for Discussion

How do you think Washington felt about leading the Continental Army? How would YOU feel if asked to lead a bunch of untrained and poorly-armed colonists against the most powerful military force in the world?!

_____

_____

_____

_____

_____

_____

The French and Indian War

Long before the colonists' fight for freedom, the countries of England and France were in a race to control the Ohio Valley. The French had begun to build a chain of forts between Lake Erie and the Ohio River. A twenty-one-year-old Virginian knew this territory well because he had surveyed land in the region. His name was George Washington. He was sent to persuade the French to stop building the forts. When they refused, he led a troop of 150 men in an attack on one of the forts. This began the French and Indian War of 1754-1763. Who was this Virginian? Why, George Washington?

Thomas Jefferson

"Goochland, Virginia was my home. I was born there in 1743. I've been a lawyer, statesman, political theorist, musician, planter, architect, and archaeologist, and I wrote the first draft of the Declaration of Independence. In 1801, I became America's third president. I enlarged America through the Louisiana Purchase, and sent Meriwether Lewis and William Clark on their famous expedition. However, I guess I'm most proud of founding the University of Virginia. An education is essential, you know. My name is THOMAS JEFFERSON."

Thomas Jefferson wrote the Declaration of Independence and the Virginia Statute for Religious Freedom. He also founded the University of Virginia and served as the President of the United States. Thomas Jefferson provided political leadership by expressing the reasons for colonial independence from England in the Declaration of Independence.

More Reasons Why the Colonists Wanted Independence

- King George was the only person who could approve or reject laws. (Sometimes this took years)
- Royal Governors forced colonial legislatures to meet in inconvenient places.
- King George kept colonists from moving west of the Appalachians.
- King George forced colonists to provide places for British soldiers to stay.

Thomas Jefferson was a Virginian who served in the House of Burgesses, as his father had before him. Jefferson's father died when he was only 14 years old, leaving him to run a large farm with 30 slaves. In 1760 he enrolled at the College of William and Mary in Williamsburg, from which he graduated two years later at the age of 19. After getting his degree, he studied law and was admitted to the bar in 1767. His great skill was in the written word. Other burgesses often asked Thomas Jefferson to write laws and resolutions for them. Later he was asked to write America's Declaration of Independence!

1. The Declaration of Independence stated that the people wanted:

A. to go back home to England   B. to stop fighting   C. freedom

Hard to believe but true

The Continental Congress debated Jefferson's first draft. A few passages, including one condemning King George for encouraging the slave trade, were removed. On July 4, 1776, the congress approved the final draft, and members of the congress approved the Declaration of Independence.

Question for Classroom Discussion

The Declaration of Independence means different things to different people. For Americans today, it is an important national symbol. Pretend that you were there July 4, 1776. The Declaration of Independence is brand new! What would it mean to you if you were a...

- Colonist
- British soldier
- Slave on a Virginia plantation
- Signer of the Declaration of Independence
- Royal governor appointed by King George III

Background check

These Virginia delegates signed the Declaration of Independence. Look them up and learn more about them.

Carter Braxton

Benjamin Harrison

Thomas Jefferson

Francis Lightfoot Lee

Richard Henry Lee

Thomas Nelson, Jr.

George Wythe

Patrick Henry

"I was born in 1736 in Hanover County, Virginia. I became a member of the House of Burgesses and both Continental Congresses. I became known as a great speaker. I became governor of the new commonwealth of Virginia as soon as it was established in 1776. I was a leader in adding the Bill of Rights to the U.S. Constitution. My name is PATRICK HENRY."

Patrick Henry inspired patriots from other colonies when he spoke out against taxation without representation by saying:

"I know not what course others may take; but as for me, give me liberty, or give me death!"

1. Patrick Henry is best known as a:

    A. Writer

    B. Speaker

    C. Patriot

    D. B and C

How did good writing and speaking skills help early Virginia leaders achieve their goals?

Write your ideas here:

The last major battle of the Revolutionary War was fought in 1781 at Yorktown, Virginia. The American victory resulted in the surrender of the English army, bringing an end to the war.

The war continued in parts of the colonies for two more years. The British began peace talks with the Americans in 1782, and a peace treaty was finally signed in 1783.

The French navy helped George Washington by guarding Chesapeake Bay. The ships kept any British troops from leaving or landing at Yorktown. The French ships and American soldiers worked together to defeat the British army.

What Virginia water feature was important to the British surrender at Yorktown, Virginia?

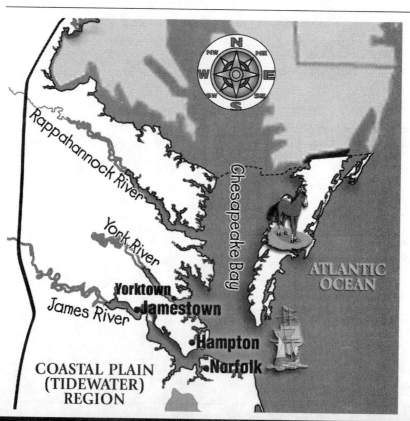

Hard-To-Believe-But-True!
The British surrender at Yorktown took place on October 19, 1781. More than 8,000 men laid down their arms as a British band reportedly played a tune called "The World Turned Upside Down." The troops represented about a fourth of Britain's military force in America.

Here We Go Again!

You, a Virginia colonist, are in a great debate with your English friend. She just cannot understand why you no longer want to be part of England. Put a V by your comments. Put an E by the comments she made.

☐ "I want the right to worship the way in which I choose, not the way some government tells me I will."

☐ "You are represented in your government, and I want the same privilege — especially if I have to pay taxes to that government."

☐ "My country established the Virginia colony and you are under English rule."

☐ "England can govern the colonies; it doesn't matter that we're all the way across the Atlantic Ocean from you."

☐ "Our Declaration of Independence will take care of this matter."

Here are some books about life in colonial America for you to enjoy!

Johnny Tremain, by Esther Forbes

The "Felicity" Series, by Valerie Tripp

Book of the American Colonies, by Howard Egger-Bovet and Marlene Smith-Baranzini; part of the Brown Paper School US Kids History Series

A Revolutionary Enrichment Exercise!

Number the events below in the order in which they happened during the Revolutionary era.

Washington crosses the Delaware to fight the British

☐

Patrick Henry says...

Give me LIBERTY ... or give me DEATH!

☐

Thomas Jefferson writes the Declaration of Independence

☐

George Washington is sworn in as our first president

☐

A Quick Review for YOU!

Match the people on the left with the fact about them on the right.

_____ 1. George Washington   A. Inspired patriots with famous speech

_____ 2. Thomas Jefferson   B. Commander-in-Chief of Continental Army

_____ 3. Patrick Henry   C. Expressed reasons for colonial independence

There's one thing about our founding fathers. They weren't ones to say, "I can't."

If you had been in Virginia during this revolutionary era when the nation was being formed, what would you have agreed to give a try?

❏ Write a long, important document
❏ Serve as president
❏ Be in charge of the army
❏ Attend a convention
❏ Make a speech

Find and list a reason why Americans wanted independence from Great Britain.

_____

_____

_____

In September 1776, Jefferson resigned from Congress and returned to the Virginia House of Delegates. He had no interest in military life and did not fight in the Revolutionary War. He felt that he could be more useful in Virginia as a lawmaker.

leadership: the ability to guide, direct, or influence people

Below is a list of everyone who signed the Declaration of Independence! See if you can find all these people in the Word Search! Look closely — words go in all directions!

Massachusetts
John Hancock
Samuel Adams
John Adams
Robert Treat Paine
Elbridge Gerry
New Hampshire
Josiah Bartlett
William Whipple
Matthew Thornton
Rhode Island
Stephen Hopkins
William Ellery

Connecticut
Roger Sherman
Samuel Huntington
William Williams
Oliver Wolcott
New York
William Floyd
Philip Livingston
Francis Lewis
Lewis Morris
New Jersey
Richard Stockton
John Witherspoon
Francis Hopkinson

John Hart
Abraham Clark
Pennsylvania
Robert Morris
Benjamin Rush
Benjamin Franklin
John Morton
George Clymer
James Smith
George Taylor
James Wilson
George Ross
Delaware
Caesar Rodney

George Read
Thomas McKean
Maryland
Samuel Chase
William Paca
Thomas Stone
Charles Carrol
Virginia
George Wythe
Richard Henry Lee
Thomas Jefferson
Benjamin Harrison
Thomas Nelson, Jr.
Francis Lightfoot Lee

Carter Braxton
North Carolina
William Hooper
Joseph Hewes
John Penn
South Carolina
Edward Rutledge
Thomas Heyward , Jr.
Thomas Lynch, Jr.
Arthur Middleton
Georgia
Button Gwinnett
Lyman Hall
George Walton

```
N O T K C O T S D R A H C I R E G A N K Z S E I O N B D A H D B N S S R P
I O Q H Y E I L J E S E T H N S R E N D T P F M O W U U U K A E O A I I D
B X T T O J G O L A U H L I A T E O O E N O F T P D T H Y E E N S M R C P
D F G G D M H D M A O F A B H R O W P R Z D X X Y X T D I Y R J L U R H K
H G R E N N A U E M H P F U R P L H E D G A X O E E O N W B E A I E O A B
Y S R K A I E S A L T N R R S I E E V H R E L I G M N K B N G M W L M R I
N N U D F L T S J A T M A R A N D Z S B H F R E X E G R K O R I S A S D D
M O A R C N L N E E I U E M H N B G R C M P O O P S W O F T O N E D I H R
E M T H N Y O R U D F H R O Y E C E E A A R E N S M I B R S E F M A W E E
S T A R N I T T D H T F P D N L T I I G G R H S T S N E S G G R A M E N M
K S A C O T M L N I L K E J R R K L S E E O R J O Y N R M N N A J S L R Y
E Y H J R M E A W R I E A R A A L R W L J R T O R J E T A I A N E A J Y L
E J L E E T N N J N O M U C S I W Y A D I R R X L X T M I V M K L W M L C
R Y B H O R H H S N I H X M W O T D Z L G G K Y Q L T O L I R L P I H E E
M O L N D O D A O N E S T D A H N H E F C E H U Q Y B R L L E I P L W E G
R L H J J A I U H J T B K W E S T F O T Y M O T R Q W R I P H N I L I J R
J O S I A H B A R T L E T T E Q M Q M M B E A R F U U I W I S T H I L A O
A T V R R D R N O S N I K P O H S I C N A R F H G O T S M L R R W A L M E
Y E N D O R R A S E A C R R N B T U J Q D S N K A E O X A I E A M M I E G
W I L L I A M E L L E R Y P Q B J T D M J A M O G R W T I H G H A H A S F
L A A S R J N O S L E N S A M O H T A O N O H C I Q B A L P O N I O M S W
T H O M A S H E Y W A R D J R P F A F M O Q C W K Z L A L E R H L O P M R
E N O T S S A M O H T M T T O C L O W R E V I L O E K I I T E O L P A I Q
Z V T R K M E K F R A N C I S L E W I S I G J R J Z A B W H O J I E C T U
G E O R G E T A Y L O R F W L T G K J K K C O C N A H N H O J N W R A H C
```

Section 3

Political Growth and Western Expansion 1781 to the Mid-1800s

In 1775, Daniel Boone blazed the Wilderness Road through the Cumberland Gap. From 1775 to 1800, thousands of Pioneers

travelled through the gap as a passage westward into the Cumberland Mountains and the Appalachian Plateau.

Chapter 5

VS.6a — Virginia played an important role in the establishment of the new American nation. Correlates with VS.1a, VS.1c, VS.1d, and VS.1g.

Father of Our Country

George Washington, a Virginian, was elected as the first President of the United States of America. He provided the strong leadership needed to help the young country and provided a model of leadership for future presidents. That is why he is called the "Father of Our Country."

Hard-to-Believe-But-True

During the American Revolution, George Washington refused pay for serving as Commander-in-Chief of the Continental Army!

Background Check!

Thomas Jefferson wrote this description of Washington's character:

"He was, indeed, in every sense of the words, a wise, a good and a great man.... On the whole, his character was, in its mass, perfect... it may truly be said, that never did nature and fortune combine more perfectly to make a man great...."

thomas jefferson

George Mercer, a friend of Washington's, wrote this description of him:

"He may be described as being straight as an Indian, measuring 6 feet 2 inches in his stockings, and weighing 175 pounds... A large and straight rather than a prominent nose; blue-gray penetrating eyes.... He has a clear though rather colorless pale skin which burns with the sun... dark brown hair which he wears in a queue.... His mouth is large and generally firmly closed, but which from time to time discloses some defective teeth.... His movements and gestures are graceful, his walk majestic, and he is a splendid horseman."

george mercer

queue: a short braid of hair worn at the back of the neck by soldiers and sailors in the late 1700s and early 1800s

James Madison

James Madison was called the "Father of the Constitution." He also was the fourth President of the United States.

"I was born in Port Conway, Virginia in 1751. I was a delegate to the Constitutional Convention and helped draft Virginia's constitution. I was honored by being called the "Father of the Constitution." I played a big role in creating the Bill of Rights. In 1801, I became U.S. Secretary of State, and from 1809-1817, I served as America's fourth president. My name is JAMES MADISON."

James Madison believed in the importance of having a United States Constitution. He kept detailed notes during the Constitutional Convention. His skills at compromise helped the delegates reach agreement during the difficult process of writing the Constitution of the United States of America. This earned him the title "Father of the Constitution."

1. Why is James Madison called the "Father of the Constitution"?

A. His skills at compromise helped the delegates reach agreement.

B. His skills at constitutionize helped the delegates reach agreement.

C. His skills at improvise helped the delegates reach agreement.

D. He did not have any skills at reaching a compromise.

2. Washington and Madison were both founding "fathers." How were they similar? How were they different?

_____

_____

_____

George Mason and the Virginia Declaration of Rights

The Virginia Declaration of Rights, written by George Mason, states that all Virginians should have certain rights, including freedom of religion and freedom of the press. The document became the basis for the Bill of Rights of the Constitution of the United States of America.

"I was born in Fairfax County, Virginia in 1725. I preferred to work behind the scenes and refused many public offices. I became a member of the second Virginia Convention in Richmond in 1775. I also attended the third Virginia Convention in Williamsburg in 1776, where I wrote the Declaration of Rights and a large part of the state constitution. My name is George Mason."

Thomas Jefferson used Mason's Declaration of Rights when he wrote the Declaration of Independence. James Madison also used Mason's ideas in 1789 when he drafted the 10 constitutional amendments that became the Bill of Rights.

In 1787, George Mason played an important role in the Constitutional Convention, but he refused to sign the final draft of the United States Constitution because it did not contain a bill of rights.

The basis for the United States Bill of Rights was...

A. The United States Constitution

B. The Virginia Declaration of Rights

C. The Declaration of Independence

Virginia Statute for Religious Freedom

- Separated church and state and established religious freedom
- Basis for the First Amendment to the U.S. Constitution, which guarantees freedom of religion

The Virginia Statute for Religious Freedom, written by Thomas Jefferson, states that all people should be free to worship as they please. This document was the basis for the First Amendment to the Constitution of the United States of America, the amendment that protects religious freedom.

Number which document came first in each pair below.

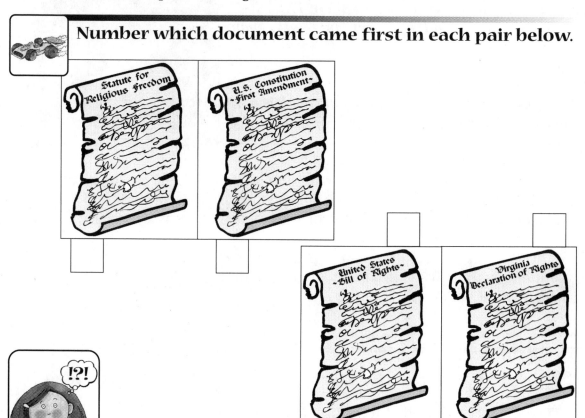

Jefferson was proud of writing the Virginia Statute for Religious Freedom. The inscription that Jefferson wrote for his grave marker reads: "Here was buried Thomas Jefferson, Author of the Declaration of American Independence, of the Statute of Virginia for religious freedom, & Father of the University of Virginia." He ranked those accomplishments higher than being president of the United States!

A Quick Review for YOU!

Match the people on the left with the fact about them on the right.

_____ 1. George Washington   A. Said, "Give me liberty or give me death."

_____ 2. Thomas Jefferson   B. "Father of Our Country"

_____ 3. James Madison   C. Wrote the Virginia Statute for Religious Freedom

_____ 4. George Mason   D. "Father of the Constitution"

_____ 5. Patrick Henry   E. Wrote the Virginia Declaration of Rights

A Quick Review for YOU!

Each of the four documents shown here was significant in establishing the rights of Virginians and Americans.

Match each document to one of the things it accomplished.

A — Declaration of Independence

B — Virginia Declaration of Rights

C — Statute for Religious Freedom

D — The Virginia Company Charter

1   Formed the basis of the Bill of Rights

2   Declared freedom from English rule

3   Extended English rights to colonists

4   Separated church and state

A ☐   B ☐   C ☐   D ☐

The Louisiana Purchase

In 1803, a large tract of land was bought from France. This purchase almost doubled the size of the United States! This expanse of land extended roughly from the Mississippi River to the Rocky Mountains and from New Orleans, Louisiana to the Canadian border. This acquisition changed America from a small nation to a large one overnight. As colonists moved into the new territory, they were drawn westward even past the Rockies, all the way to the Pacific Ocean!

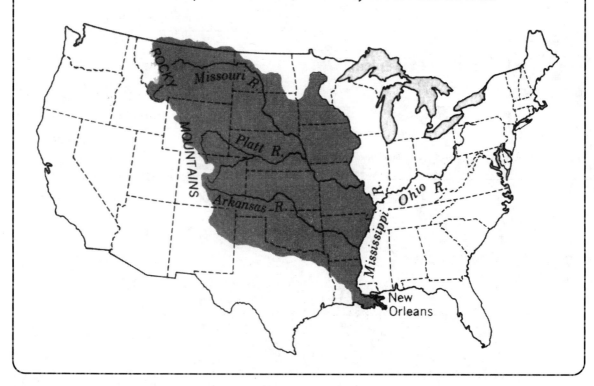

Westward, Ho!

After the American Revolution, Virginia's agricultural base began to change; as a result, large numbers of Virginians moved west and to the deep South to find better farmland and new opportunities. Geography influenced the movement of people and ideas as Virginians moved to and beyond the Virginia frontier.

Land Sakes!

Tobacco farming is hard on the soil. Growing tobacco uses up the nutrients in the soil. After a few years, nothing will grow. It can take years for the soil to build up the nutrients needed to grow another crop.

Because of this situation, many farmers to looked west and south for new land to farm. Virginians migrated into western territories looking for large areas of land and new opportunities.

 What geographic factors caused Virginians to move to the western frontier of Virginia and beyond? (Check all that apply.)

_____ A. There was better farmland to the west and south of Virginia

_____ B. Tobacco farming had robbed the soil of nutrients

_____ C. Tobacco farmers were using all the farmland

_____ D. Farmers wanted a vacation

_____ E. All of the above

 What is the effect of growing the same crop (like tobacco) year after year?

_____

Head for the Gap!

Settlers crossed the Appalachian Mountains through the Cumberland Gap as they migrated to new lands in the west. The Cumberland Gap is a pass in the Appalachian Mountains where Kentucky, Tennessee, and Virginia meet. The gap is a 600-foot-deep notch in the Cumberland Mountains.

In 1775, the famous pioneer Daniel Boone blazed the Wilderness Road through the gap. The Wilderness Road was an important pioneer road. Daniel Boone and a party of woodsmen began to cut a trail. Their route began at the Holston River in what is now Tennessee, passed through the Powell River Valley, crossed the Cumberland Mountains through Cumberland Gap, and ended in present-day Kentucky.

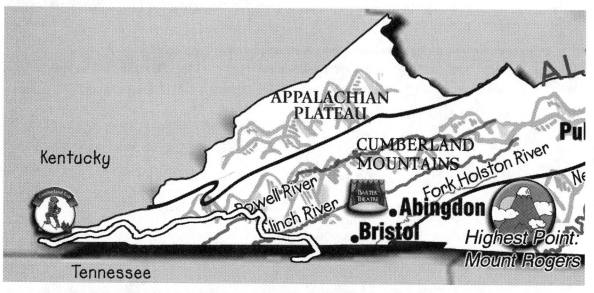

 Why did the Wilderness Road run through the Cumberland Gap?

_____

_____

_____

Don't Leave Your Culture Behind!

As Virginians moved into the western territories, they took their traditions, ideas, and cultures with them. Native Americans, British, and other European immigrants influenced Virginia's culture.

Culture is a way of life. When we talk about culture we might mean ideas, traditions, inventions, language, technology, values, music, or art! Culture is not something a person is born with. It's something that is learned by speaking with and listening to others.

culture: the general behavior and lifestyle of a group of people

Question for Discussion

Compare and contrast the first Virginians who settled at Jamestown with the first Virginians who crossed the Cumberland Gap. Did they have similar or different…

• *Cultures?*
• *Ideas?*
• *Traditions?*
• *Hardships?*
• *Needs?*
• *Goals?*

What does culture mean?

_____ A. Behavior of a group

_____ B. Lifestyle of a group

_____ C. Both of these

Geographic factors influenced Virginians to move to the western frontier.

After the American Revolution, Virginians were able to move west past the Appalachian Mountains. There were already other colonies to the north and south, and the Atlantic Ocean lay to the east. There was no other place for Virginians to claim new land but west!

THE UNITED STATES, 1787

A Quick Review For You!

1. What crop was hard on the soil and forced farmers to look for fresh land?

   _____ A. Wheat

   _____ B. Tobacco

   _____ C. Barley

2. What were Virginians looking for in western territories?

   _____ A. Large areas of land and new opportunities

   _____ B. Small areas of land and old opportunities

   _____ C. Swamplands and no opportunities

3. When Virginians moved, what did they take with them?

   _____ A. Tractors, ID cards, and catchers

   _____ B. Traditions, ideas, and cultures

   _____ C. Tobacco, ID cards, and vultures

4. What did settlers who crossed the Appalachian Mountains

   travel through?

   _____ A. Cumberland Gap

   _____ B. Cucumber Gap

   _____ C. Cummerbund Gap

5. Geographic factors influenced Virginians to move to the western frontier

   of Virginia and beyond.

   _____ A. True

   _____ B. False

Background Check: Fashion

Colonists dressed much as they had back in England. Working men wore knee-length breeches with long stockings, shirts, and vests. Women wore skirts called petticoats and blouses. They tied a pouch on a string around their waist over their apron to serve as a "pocket." Women generally wore mob caps of white cloth, often beneath a straw hat. Women wore hats indoors and out. In Williamsburg, you might have seen men in wigs wearing three-cornered cocked (tricorn) hats. These were often decorated with ostrich plumes or pheasant feathers and colorful ribbon rosettes called cockades. Children dressed much like adults! (Don't you think they would have liked tee shirts!)

Draw a line from each word to its correct place on the characters.

Petticoat

Tricorn hat

Mob cap

Blouse

Stockings

Apron

Wig

Breeches

Section 4

Civil War and Post-War Eras

Virginians were divided about secession from the Union. This division led to the creation of West Virginia. After receiving approval from the U.S. Congress and President Abraham Lincoln, West Virginia was admitted to the Union as the 35th state on June 20, 1863.

Chapter 6

VS.7a — Differences between Northern and Southern states divided Virginians and led to secession, war, and the creation of West Virginia.
Correlates with VS.1a, VS.1b, VS.1c, VS.1d, VS.1e, VS.1f, VS.1g, and VS.1i

Conflict Leads to Crisis!

After the Revolutionary War, conflicts arose between the northern and southern states over states' rights and slavery. These same conflicts occurred within Virginia.

The North and the South had different economies:
- The economy in the northern part of the United States was industrialized.
- The economy in the southern part of the United States was agricultural and relied on slave labor

Circle your answer:

1. Which scene represents the economy of the North at the time of the Civil War?:
A or B

2. Which scene represents the basis of the economy in the southern states at the time of the Civil War?:
A or B

The northern and southern states took different positions over the expansion of slavery into the new territories.

slave state: a state where the ownership of slaves is legal
free state: a state where the ownership of slaves is not legal

• Northern states wanted any new states to be "free states."
• Southern states wanted any new states to be "slave states."

The disagreement became so heated that southern states wanted to secede (withdraw) from the United States.

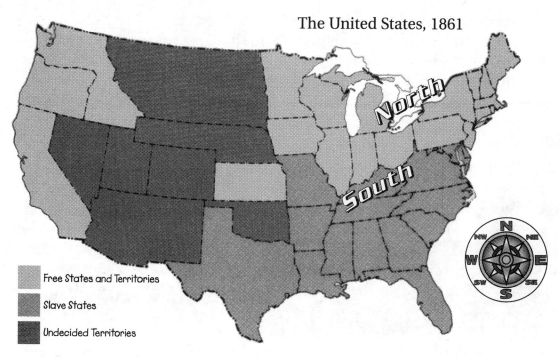

The United States, 1861

□ Free States and Territories
■ Slave States
■ Undecided Territories

1. Which states on the map above were in favor of slavery and secession?:

___North ___South

2. Which states were in favor of abolition and preserving the Union?:

abolition: to do away with something; abolitionists wanted to do away with slavery

___South ___North

3. How many undecided territories were there in 1861? _____

Virginians were divided about secession from the Union, which led to the creation of West Virginia. Conflicts arose between the eastern counties that relied on slavery and the western counties that favored the abolition of slavery.

After receiving approval from the U.S. Congress and President Abraham Lincoln, West Virginia was admitted to the Union as the 35th state on June 20, 1863.

Virginia before split

Virginia and West Virginia after split

1. Which side of Virginia was in favor of slavery?:   __East __West
2. Which side of Virginia was against slavery?:   __West __East

Question for Discussion
How would you feel about secession if you had been a citizen of a...
- *Southern State*
- *Northern State*

Events Leading to Secession and War

Abolitionists wanted to see slaves go free. They campaigned to end slavery. Nat Turner and John Brown brought national attention to the abolitionist movement. Nat Turner led a revolt against plantation owners in Virginia. This was known as Nat Turner's Rebellion. John Brown led a raid on the United States Armory (Arsenal) at Harpers Ferry, Virginia. He was trying to start a slave rebellion. He was captured and hanged.

Harriet Tubman

Harriet Tubman was an African-American woman who escaped from slavery. She established a secret route that escaped slaves took; it became known as the "Underground Railroad." The Underground Railroad was neither underground, nor a railroad. It was a secret group of people who helped slaves escape to freedom.

Harriet Tubman made many trips to the South. She had help from other people along the Underground Railroad. She was known as the "Moses of Her People," after the Biblical figure that led the Jews from slavery in Egypt.

Harriet Tubman became a famous "conductor" on the Underground Railroad. She was never caught and she never lost a "passenger." There was a $40,000 reward for Harriet's capture — dead or alive!

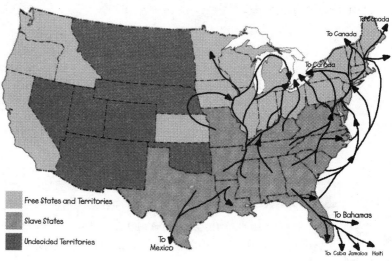

Free States and Territories

Slave States

Undecided Territories

To Canada

To Canada

To Canada

To Bahamas

To Mexico

To Cuba Jamaica Haiti

The success of the Underground Railroad was another factor leading to secession and war.

1. What areas did escaped slaves travel away from?

_____

2. What areas did escaped slaves travel to?

_____

3. Did slaves travel through Virginia?

_____

4. Was Virginia a slave state or a free state?

_____

The South Secedes! Virginia Secedes!

Because of economic differences between the North and South, the states were unable to resolve their conflicts and the South seceded from the Union.

secession: to pull away from; to leave

The Civil War

Because the North and South could not resolve their conflicts, they fought one another in the Civil War. The issues that they were fighting over were:

- States' rights: the right of a state to decide for itself what it wants to do
- Slavery
- Preservation of the Union

The Election of Lincoln

In 1860, Abraham Lincoln was elected president of the United States. Lincoln was against slavery. By the time he actually took office, seven southern states had already seceded from the Union. They not only wanted to preserve the institution of slavery, but also wanted the right to make their own laws without interference from the federal government.

These states formed a separate government. They called this government the Confederate States of America. Lincoln insisted that secession was illegal. He swore that he would protect federal possessions located in the South.

Virginia seceded from the Union on April 17, 1861 and joined the Confederacy on April 25, 1861.

Number the events below in the order in which they occurred.

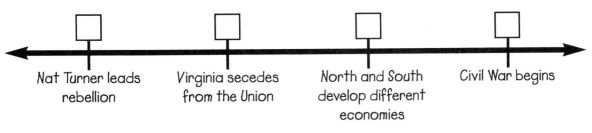

Nat Turner leads rebellion

Virginia secedes from the Union

North and South develop different economies

Civil War begins

~ This book is not reproducible. ~

Match the cause with its effect:

____ 1. North and South unable to agree
____ 2. President Lincoln calls out troops
____ 3. Western counties against slavery

A. West Virginia formed
B. Virginia and southern states secede
C. Civil War fought

A Quick Review for YOU!

1. Conflicts over slavery and other issues arose between:

    A. Northern and Southern states
    B. Eastern Virginia and western Virginia
    C. Both A and B
    D. Neither A nor B

2. A person in favor of freeing slaves was called a/an:

    A. secessionist   B. abolitionist   C. preservationist

3. The Civil War was fought over:

    A. slavery   B. states' rights   C. Union preservation
    D. All of the above

4. Nat Turner and John Brown helped slaves:

    A. revolt   B. secede   C. form a new state

5. Compare the South's secession to the Declaration of Independence.

How was it similar?: _____

How was it different?: _____

The Civil War in Virginia

After Virginia seceded from the United States, the capital of the Confederacy was moved to Richmond, Virginia. Much of the Civil War was fought in Virginia.

The first battle of the Civil War was fought at Manassas, Virginia on **Bull Run Creek**. General Thomas "Stonewall" Jackson played a major role in this battle, which the Confederacy won.

General Robert E. Lee, commander of the Army of Northern Virginia, defeated Union troops at **Fredericksburg**.

Richmond fell to Union General Ulysses S. Grant and was burned near the end of the war.

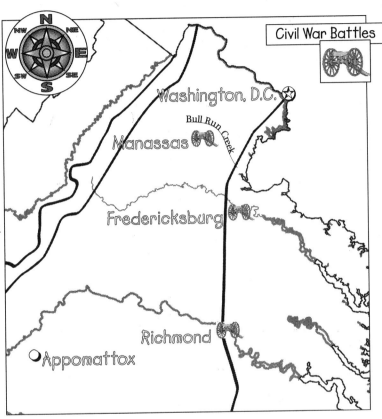

Answer the following questions using the map.

1. Which battle was closest to Washington D.C.? _____

2. Richmond (capital of the Confederacy) is _____ north or _____ south of Washington D.C.

3. Appomattox is _____ east or _____ west of Richmond.

Virginians Lead the Confederacy!

Many Virginians were leaders in the Confederate army and played a significant role in the Civil War.

Robert E. Lee:
• Commanded the Confederate Army during the Civil War
• He was offered command of the Union forces at the beginning of the Civil War, but he resigned rather than fight against his native state of Virginia.

resign: to give up or quit, as in to quit your job, or to give up a position of responsibility

J.E.B. Stuart:
• He also resigned from the United States Army to join the Confederate Army.
• Called the "eyes of the Army" by Robert E. Lee

Thomas "Stonewall" Jackson:
• A general in the Confederate Army
• Earned the nickname "Stonewall" at the Battle of Bull Run

The War Ends

The Civil War ended at Appomattox Court House, Virginia. It was here that General Robert E. Lee surrendered his army to Union General Ulysses S. Grant.

surrender: to give up, as in to give up to an enemy force

Virginia in the Civil War

Number the events below in the order in which they occurred.

☐   ☐   ☐   ☐

| Lee takes command of Confederate Army | Lee surrenders to Grant at Appomattox | Richmond named Confederate capital | Confederacy wins first battle at Manassas |

Standing Like a Stone Wall!

Legend says that General Thomas Jackson was so steadfast in battle that he was compared to a "stone wall." That is how he got his nickname, "Stonewall."

Match the person on the left with their Civil War role on the right:

1. J.E.B. Stuart
2. Thomas "Stonewall" Jackson
3. Robert E. Lee

A. Served as the "eyes" of the Confederate Army
B. Commander of the Confederate Army
C. General at the Battle of Bull Run

In an encyclopedia, look up the Civil War.

1. When was the Battle of Bull Run fought?

_____

2. On what date did the Civil War end at Appomattox Court House?

_____

resign   surrender   command   battle

Use the words above
to fill in the blanks below.

1. I think I would _____ before I would fight against my own state.

2. It is hard to imagine what it was like during the _____ at Bull Run Creek near Manassas during the Civil War.

3. A general's job is to take _____ during a battle.

4. It must have been difficult for General Lee to _____ his army to General Grant.

Naval Blockade!

Abraham Lincoln was president of the United States during the Civil War. He used the Union Navy to blockade important southern

blockade: patrolling of an enemy country's coasts by warships to prevent them from receiving weapons, ammunition, reinforcements, or food from other countries

ports including Mobile, Alabama, and Wilmington, North Carolina.

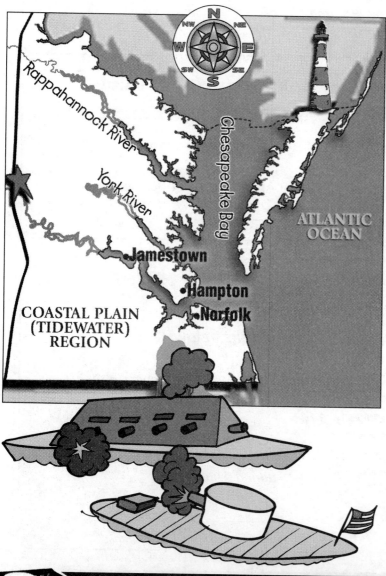

Battle of the Ironclads

On March 8, 1862, the Confederate ironclad ship named the *Merrimack* sank two Union ships at Hampton Roads, Virginia, and ran three others aground. The *Merrimack* returned the next day to finish the job, but it found a Union ironclad, the *Monitor*, waiting.

The two ships battled for more than three hours. However, their bullets had little effect on each other, and the battle ended in a draw. Within the year, however, both ships were lost. The *Merrimack* was destroyed to keep it from being captured by the Union. The *Monitor* filled with water and sank while being towed at sea in a storm.

A Quick Review for You!

1. The capital of the Confederacy was moved to Richmond
   __before __after   Virginia seceded from the Union.

2. Much of the Civil War was fought in Virginia because:

    A. General Lee lived there   B. There were creeks and stone walls
    C. of the location of Richmond and Washington, D.C.

3. Who won the first battle of the Civil War?

    A. The Union Army   B. The Confederate Army

4. Why was Thomas Jackson called "Stonewall"?

    _____

    _____

5. The Civil War ended at:

    A. Washington, D.C.   B. Appomattox Court House
    C. Richmond, Virginia   D. Manassas, Virginia

Hard-To-Believe-But-True!

The Merrimack (sometimes spelled Merrimac) originally was a wooden ship. After the Civil War began, Union troops sank it when they evacuated the Navy yard at Portsmouth, Virginia. Confederate forces raised the ship and covered it with iron plates. They renamed it Virginia, though it is often referred to by its original name.

Chapter 7

VS.8a — Reconstruction affected life in Virginia.
Correlates with VS.1b, VS.1d, VS.1e, VS.1f, and VS.1g.

Reconstruction — No Fun for Anyone!

The period following the end of the Civil War was called Reconstruction. Life was very difficult for Virginians during the Reconstruction Period. Virginians had to rebuild the state after the Civil War. The U.S. Congress passed laws designed to rebuild the country and bring the Southern states back into the Union. Virginia was readmitted to the Union on January 26, 1870.

Virginians had many problems to solve following the Civil War.

- Millions of newly freed slaves needed food, clothing, shelter, and jobs.
- Virginia's economy was in ruins:
  - Confederate money had no value.
  - Banks were closed.
  - Railroads, bridges, plantations, and crops were destroyed from the war.

Match the problem below with the effect it had.

1. No government

2. Banks closed

3. Destroyed crops

A. Hunger and starvation

B. No one in charge

C. No way to buy anything

Virginians Rebuild!

As Virginians identified the many problems they had to solve, they began to come up with responses and solutions. Some of these were:

- The U.S. Congress created the Freedman's Bureau that provided food, schools, and medical care for freed slaves and others in Virginia and the rest of the South.

- Because plantation owners (slaveholders) did not have money to pay workers, and because former slaves needed land and work, sharecropping developed. Sharecropping let freedmen and poor white farmers rent land from a landowner by promising to pay the owner with a share of the crop.

- Virginia adopted a new state constitution that banned slavery and gave African-American men the right to vote.

- People moved from the countryside to cities in search of economic opportunities.

 ## Answer the following questions:

1. The Freedman's Bureau was created to help:

A. Congress   B. freed slaves
C. plantation owners D. bridge builders

2. What type of opportunity might a Virginian who moved to the city from the countryside during the Reconstruction Period have found?

A. sharecropping   B. construction job   C. banker

3. Plantation owners used this method to help freed slaves get back to work:

A. sharecropping   B. railroading   C. voting

4. Virginia's new state constitution:

   A. banned slavery and gave African-American men the vote
   B. forced people to move from the countryside to the city
   C. gave Confederate money value

5. As Virginians moved from the countryside to the cities, the population of cities:

   A. increased   B. decreased   C. stayed the same

The Civil War has just ended. You have been put in charge of making a plan to help freed slaves during this period of reconstruction.

What are some things you would do to help the freed slaves?

☐ Provide food

☐ Build a bridge

☐ Plan a party

☐ Build homes

☐ Provide clothing

☐ Plant crops

☐ Go swimming

A Quick Review for YOU!

1. The period following the Civil War was known as:

   A. Freedman
   B. Sharecropping
   C. Reconstruction

2. The Reconstruction Period came __before __after the Civil War.

3. Today, slavery is __illegal __legal in Virginia.

4. Confederate money was __worthless __valuable following the Civil War.

One More For Fun

Pretend you lived during Reconstruction. How would your life have changed during the time period after the Civil War if you had been a…

Former Slave	Former Slaveholder
_____	_____
_____	_____
_____	_____
_____	_____
_____	_____
_____	_____

Segregation in Virginia

The practice of segregation had a significant impact on life in Virginia. Segregation meant that people in Virginia were segregated, or divided, by race. Because of this, African Americans established their own churches, businesses, and schools.

During Reconstruction, African Americans began to have some power in Virginia's government. Men of all races could vote. However, these gains were reversed when laws were passed that made it difficult for African Americans to vote and hold office. These laws imposed poll taxes and literacy tests. In other words, if African Americans could not pay the poll tax or pass the literacy test, they were not allowed to vote or hold office.

Even though black families wanted to better themselves, segregation put up many barriers to any hope of success. In spite of the efforts of blacks, many whites continued to discriminate against them. Virginia, like most of the South, was divided along racial lines.

discrimination: an unfair difference in the treatment of people

Jim Crow Laws

Certain laws, called Jim Crow laws, discriminated against African Americans in Virginia and other Southern states. These laws also reinforced prejudices held by white people about black people.

Under these Jim Crow laws, African Americans were not allowed to:
- Ride in the same section of buses and trains as whites
- Eat in the same restaurants as whites
- Attend the same public schools as white citizens
- Drink from the same drinking fountains as white citizens

These laws also had an impact on the economic life of African Americans. For example, it was legal for an employer to pay black workers less money than white workers were paid.

Answer the following questions about segregation and Jim Crow laws.

1. An example of segregation is:

    A. Not being able to go to the bank
    B. Not being allowed to go to the same school as white children
    C. Not being able to travel to another state

2. The result of Jim Crow laws and segregation was:

    A. discrimination   B. literacy   C. employment

3. A poll tax and literacy test often kept African Americans from:

    A. eating   B. riding   C. voting

4. Under Jim Crow laws, white employers were legally allowed to pay African Americans __ more __ less than they paid white workers.

5. Segregation divided black and white Virginians by:

    A. age   B. race   C. gender

Can you think of a time when someone discriminated against you?

_____

_____

How would you have felt...?

· If you were not allowed to go to the same school as other children in your community?

· If you did the same job but were paid less money?

· If you could not eat at the same restaurant as other people?

· If you were not allowed to vote because of your race?

Number these events in the correct order.

☐ Jim Crow laws   ☐ Civil War

☐ Reconstruction   ☐ Slavery is legal

Which of the following is an example of prejudice?

A. "You can't play sports because you are a girl!"

B. "You are not as good as me because your skin is a different color!"

C. "You are too old to do that job!"

D. All of the above

 ©2002 Carole Marsh/Gallopade International • 800-536-2GET • www.virginiaexperience.com • Page 124
~ This book is not reproducible. ~

VS.8c — After the Civil War, industry and technology, transportation and cities began to grow and contribute to Virginia's economy. Virginia's cities grew with people, businesses, and factories. Correlates with VS.1d, VS.1e, VS.1f, and VS.1i.

Virginia began to grow in these areas after the Civil War and Reconstruction:

- Cities
- Factories
- Roads
- Railroads
- Coal
- Tobacco

!?! Hard-To-Believe-But-True
The world's first successful electric railway was located in Richmond in 1888.

Railroads

Railroads were a key to expansion of business, agriculture, and industry. Railroads helped small towns grow into larger cities. Railroad centers stimulated the growth of factories. These cities grew with people, businesses, and factories.

Railroads made it easy to transport natural resources (such as cotton or wood) to factories. Factories then shipped finished goods (such as clothing or furniture) to customers. Factories could make useful items such as clothing or furniture quickly.

Roanoke became a railroad center. Richmond, Norfolk, and Newport News were bustling with activity as the railroad brought new jobs and people to the areas. Petersburg, Alexandria, and Lynchburg also grew rapidly.

Write the names of two railroad centers from the map.

_____

_____

What did railroad centers stimulate the growth of?

A. Cities

B. Factories

C. Both of these

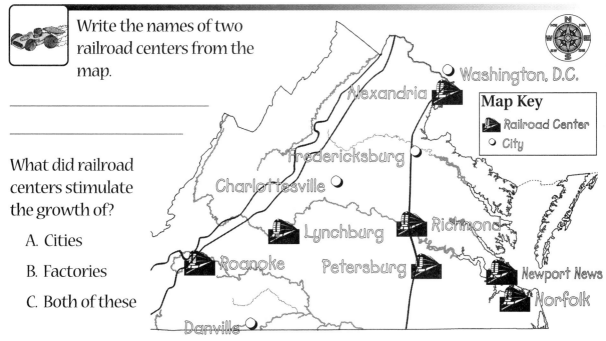

Washington, D.C.

Map Key
- Railroad Center
- City

Alexandria
Fredericksburg
Charlottesville
Lynchburg
Richmond
Roanoke
Petersburg
Newport News
Norfolk
Danville

Old King Coal

Other parts of Virginia grew as other industries developed. Coal deposits, discovered in Tazewell County after the Civil War and then in nearby counties, became a source of livelihood for residents of southwest Virginia. Coal is Virginia's most important mineral resource.

Hard-To-Believe-But-True

!?!

The first Virginia railroad began operating in 1831. The wooden track, 13 miles long, went from the coal mines of Chesterfield County to Richmond.

Old Sot Weed

Tobacco farming and tobacco products became important Virginia industries. Tobacco is grown mostly in the Piedmont region and also in the western part of the state. Tobacco is still an important crop today.

Virginia Coal Counties

Buchanan	Dickenson
Montgomery	Pulaski
Tazewell	Wise

Top Tobacco Counties

Brunswick	Pittsylvania
Halifax	Washington
Mecklenburg	

Color in the coal counties. Then use another color to fill in the tobacco counties.

Virginia on the Go!

As Virginia's cities and population grew, the need for more and better roads increased. New and improved roads were important to the development of business. Transportation routes influenced economic growth in Virginia. Railroads and interstate highways provide a way to transport goods to markets and raw materials to manufacturing centers.

A. You have just harvested your crop of apples. They need to get to market quickly before they spoil. Write an **A** in the box next to the transportation method that you could best use to achieve this goal.

B. You have mined twenty tons of coal. It is time to get it to a processing plant on the coast. Write a **B** in the box next to the transportation method that will allow you to do this most effectively.

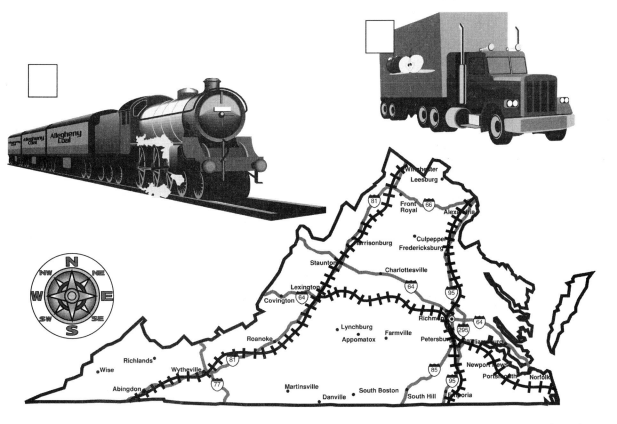

~ This book is not reproducible. ~

A Quick Review for you!

1. What did Virginia's cities do after the Civil War and Reconstruction?

    A. Grew

    B. Shrank

2. Railroads were _____ to the development of business, agriculture, and industry after the Civil War and Reconstruction.

    A. Not important

    B. Important

3. What did Virginia factories make after the Civil War and Reconstruction?

    A. Clothing

    B. Furniture

    C. Useful Items

    D. All of these

4. Which natural resource became important in Tazewell County after the Civil War and Reconstruction?

    A. Tobacco

    B. Gold

    C. Coal

5. After the Civil War and Reconstruction, Virginians needed _____ roads.

    A. More and better

    B. Fewer and narrower

    C. Fewer and better

~ This book is not reproducible. ~

6. Which were important Virginia industries after the Civil War and Reconstruction?

    A. Coal

    B. Tobacco

    C. Railroads

    D. All of these

7. Which are important Virginia industries today?

    A. Coal

    B. Tobacco

    C. Railroads

    D. All of these

8. A good way to get goods to market or raw materials to manufacturing centers:

    A. Railroads

    B. Highways

    C. Both A and B

    D. Neither A nor B

9. _____ **True or False**? Roanoke, Richmond, Norfolk, and other cities became railroad centers bustling with activity as the railroad brought new jobs and people to the area.

10. Petersburg, Alexandria, and Lynchburg _____ because of the railroads.

    A. Grew slowly

    B. Grew rapidly

    C. Did not grow

Section 5

Virginia: 1900 to the Present

Virginia Beach is the largest city in Virginia and one of the fastest-growing cities in the United States. Completed in 1941, the Pentagon, also found in Virginia, is the world's largest office building. It covers 6.5 million square feet and was built in 16 months.

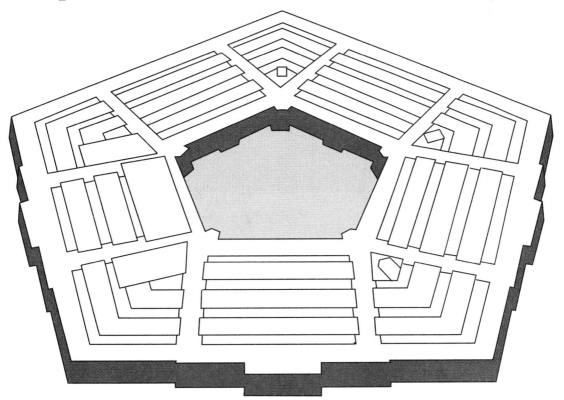

Chapter 8

VS.9a — During the twentieth century, Virginia society changed from a rural, agricultural society to a more urban, industrialized society. Correlates with VS.1b, VS.1d, VS.1e, VS.1g, and VS.1i.

Leaving the Farms for the City!

During the twentieth century, Virginia changed from a rural, agricultural society to a more urban, industrial society.

1. Match the following:

1. Rural	A. Based on farming
2. Urban	B. City
3. Agricultural	C. Based on technology
4. Industrial	D. Country

Because old systems of farming were no longer effective and crop prices were low, it became more difficult for farmers to make a living. Therefore, people began to move from the countryside to cities. This caused Virginia's cities to grow.

What were people looking for in the cities? They hoped to find economic opportunities, such as more and better jobs.

2. An example of an economic opportunity found in the city is:

A. Job with good pay and benefits

B. Company that will train you

C. Work/study program where you can earn money and improve your skills

D. All of the above

Virginia's Cities Grow!

Other factors also caused Virginia's cities to grow. These included technological developments in transportation, roads, railroads, and streetcars.

3. What caused Virginia's cities to grow in the 20th century?

A. People moving to the city from the country

B. Improved methods of farming

C. Lack of transportation

Match the cause on the left with its effect on the right.

___ 1. Old systems of farming were no longer effective

A. Sharecropping developed

___ 2. Plantation owners could not pay workers

B. It became difficult for farmers to make a living

___ 3. People could not find work in the country

C. Many people moved to the cities

A Quick Review for YOU!

Answer the following questions:

1. Railroads and streetcars are examples of:
    A. technology   B. transportation   C. trips to town

2. You are more likely to find agricultural activities in this area:
    A. rural   B. city

3. You are more likely to find industry and technology in this area:
    A. countryside   B. town/city

4. Following Reconstruction, Virginia's farmers had ___more ___less economic opportunity.

And One More for Fun!

Wow! You have lived on the farm in a small town all your life. It seems like a big decision to move to a big city. What will you do? Where will you live? How will you get around? You write a letter to your city friend and ask her all these questions. This is what she writes back to you:

_____

_____

_____

_____

_____

_____

_____

_____

_____

_____

_____

_____

_____

_____

_____

_____

_____

_____

_____

_____

_____

_____

_____

_____

_____

_____

_____

_____

_____

Welcome Home!

People have moved to Virginia from many other states and nations for jobs, freedom, and the enjoyment of Virginia's beauty and quality of life. Since the end of World War II, Northern Virginia has experienced growth due to increases in the number of federal jobs located in the region. Both Northern Virginia and the Tidewater region have grown due to computer technology.

Using the population density map below, answer the following questions:

1. This area has the lowest population density: _____

2. This area probably has a large city located in it: _____

3. This area has an average population density: _____

population density: the average number of people who live in a square mile of land

Population Density

High

Average

Low

~ This book is not reproducible. ~

The Civil Rights Movement in Virginia

During World War II, many African Americans fought for their country. When the war was over, they returned home determined to obtain their full civil rights. This campaign for equal rights is called the Civil Rights Movement. During the 20th century, Virginia struggled over the issue of civil rights.

1. Which came first?
A. The Civil Rights Movement

B. World War II

Civil rights are the privileges that you enjoy as a citizen. They can include the right to vote or an equal opportunity to get a job. For African Americans during this era, it also meant being able to sit anywhere you wanted to on a bus or being served in any restaurant.

2. Fill in the Blank: Because they had fought for their _____, African Americans believed they should have equal rights as American citizens.

In the 1950s and 1960s, African Americans began to protest against segregation and unfair laws. In Virginia, like other states across the South, began to participate in boycotts, sit-ins, and marches in order to make themselves heard and understood.

boycott: to not buy something as a way to protest

African Americans wanted to eliminate *prejudice* against them. An example of prejudice is assuming that something is true that is actually false. If you say, "All blue-eyed people are silly," you are being prejudiced. This is an unfair statement, as well as an untrue one.

sit-in: to protest something by sitting in a place and refusing to move. African Americans and others participated in boycotts and sit-ins during the Civil Rights Movement.

African Americans also fought *discrimination*. They did not believe that it was right for them to be discriminated against because of the color of their skin. For example, they did not believe that their race made any difference when it came to the jobs that they could do.

1. Check the statements you think are prejudiced:

___ A. A city person could never be a farmer.

___ B. A woman should not be a firefighter.

___ C. Someone in a wheelchair cannot be a writer.

African Americans wanted to be fully integrated into American society. White Virginians did not want to extend the civil rights that they enjoyed to African Americans. They did not like being challenged by blacks; they did not want change. Virginia governor Harry F. Byrd, Sr. led the Massive Resistance Movement against the integration of Virginia's public schools. He fought to "resist" the integration of public schools.

- **Massive Resistance**: A movement to avoid integration and continue to enforce segregation. Virginia's government established this policy. Some schools were closed to avoid integration. The policy failed and Virginia's public schools were integrated.

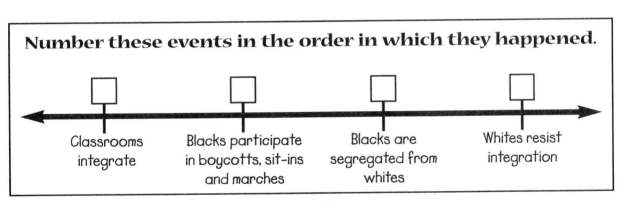

Number these events in the order in which they happened.

Classrooms integrate

Blacks participate in boycotts, sit-ins and marches

Blacks are segregated from whites

Whites resist integration

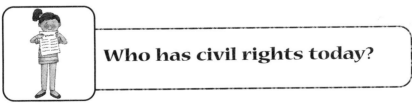

Who has civil rights today?

Brown v. Board of Education

The "separate but equal" policy tried to offer African Americans their own schools where they would be treated "equally" but continue to be "separate" from whites. The U.S. Supreme Court ruled in 1954 (*Brown v. Board of Education*) that "separate but equal" public schools were unconstitutional. All public schools were ordered to integrate. Despite widespread resistance, Virginia eventually achieved integration.

desegregation: abolishment of racial segregation

integration: full equality of all races in the use of public facilities

Question for Discussion

In 1954, all nine of the U.S. Supreme Court justices agreed that separate but equal schools were not fair. By 1960, however, several Southern states still had no black students enrolled in public schools with white students. If you lived during the 1960s, how would you feel if you were…

• *An African-American student starting at a newly integrated school*

• *The only African-American student in a new school*

• *A U.S. Supreme Court justice*

• *The Governor of Virginia*

• *A white student at a segregated school*

• *A white student at an integrated school*

• *A teacher, principal, or administrator*

A great book about one young girl's struggle for equal rights is *Roll of Thunder, Hear My Cry*, by Mildred D. Taylor.

Match the situation on the left with its likely result on the right.

1. You defend your nation in war.

2. You work against new laws.

3. You boycott a store which has unfair hiring practices.

A. Hiring practices are improved.

B. You expect equal rights when you return home.

C. Laws are upheld, despite of your efforts to fight them.

How was the Civil Rights Movement similar to Reconstruction? How was it different?

A Quick Review for YOU!

1. The period of time when many Americans worked to help African Americans obtain equal treatment is known as the:

   A. Civil Rights Movement   B. World War II   C. Massive Resistance

2. African Americans ___did ___did not want to be "separate but equal."

3. African Americans and others protested discrimination through…

   A. fighting a world war   B. boycotts and sit-ins   C. Massive Resistance

VS.9c — Many individuals contributed to the history of Virginia and the United States in the 20th century. Correlates with VS.1a and VS.1e.

Accomplished Virginians

Many individuals made great contributions to the history of our state and to the nation during the 20th century. Let's look at just a few of the people who have had such an influence on our lives.

Maggie L. Walker
- *First African-American woman to become a bank president in the United States*
- *First woman to become a bank president*

Harry F. Byrd Sr.
- *Served as governor and senator of Virginia*
- *Known for "Pay As You Go" policy for road improvements*
- *Modernized Virginia state government*

"Pay as you go" was a policy of paying for road improvements as they were made, instead of the state going into debt for such construction.

Arthur R. Ashe, Jr.
- *First African-American winner of a major men's tennis singles championship*
- *Author and eloquent spokesperson for social change*

L. Douglas Wilder
- *Served as Governor of Virginia*
- *First African American to be elected a state governor in the United States*

Who Am I?

Match the person on the left with their accomplishment on the right:

____ 1. Arthur Ashe
____ 2. Maggie Wilson
____ 3. L. Douglas Wilder
____ 4. Harry F. Byrd, Sr.

A. I was a Virginia governor and senator.
B. I was a world tennis champion.
C. I was the first African-American governor.
D. I was the first female bank president.

Choose a Virginian from the list above and pretend you are that person. A reporter is interviewing you for an article. You are asked, "What is your most important contribution to Virginia? Write your answer here.

_____

_____

_____

_____

_____

Look it up!

Learn more about these people who made important contributions to Virginia and our country.

Jane Addams	John Paul Jones	Rosa Parks	J.E.B. Stuart
Susan B. Anthony	Robert E. Lee	Pocahontas	Harriet Tubman
John Brown	James Madison	Lewis F. Powell Jr.	Nat Turner
Davy Crockett	Thurgood Marshall	Chief Powhatan	Maggie Lena Walker
Patrick Henry	George Mason	Jackie Robinson	Booker T. Washington
Thomas Jefferson	James Monroe	Captain John Smith	George Wythe

A Quick Review for You!

1. During the twentieth century, Virginia's population…

    A. Decreased

    B. Shrank

    C. Grew

2. Who was Maggie L. Walker?

    A. First woman pilot

    B. First woman bank president

    C. First woman in space

3. What was "Massive Resistance"?

    A. Resistance to integration of public schools

    B. Wind resistance

    C. Resistance to peer pressure

4. What is Desegregation?

    A. Same as segregation

    B. Abolishment of racial segregation

    C. Massive Resistance

5. Which U.S. Supreme Court case ruled segregation was unconstitutional?

    A. Brown v. Board of Education

    B. Rocky v. Drago

    C. Tyson v. Holyfield

6. Which was a road improvement policy of Governor Harry F. Byrd's?

    A. Pay Per View

    B. Pay As You Go

    C. Pay to Play

Chapter 9

VS.10a — Virginia has three branches of government. Correlates with VS.1d.

Who's in Charge Here?

Virginia state government is made up of three parts (branches) that ensure Virginia laws agree with the state constitution.

- *Legislative Branch* — The General Assembly is the legislative branch of the Virginia government that makes state laws. It is divided into two parts — the Senate and the House of Delegates.

- *Executive Branch* — The governor heads the executive branch of the state government. The executive branch makes sure that state laws are carried out.

- *Judicial Branch* — The judicial branch is the state's court system. The judicial branch decides cases about people accused of breaking laws and whether or not a law agrees with Virginia's constitution.

Each government branch has a certain job to do. Each branch also has some power over the other branches. We call this system checks and balances. The three branches work together to make our government work smoothly.

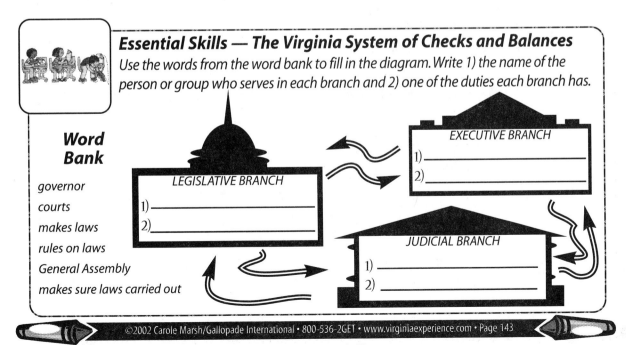

Essential Skills — The Virginia System of Checks and Balances

Use the words from the word bank to fill in the diagram. Write 1) the name of the person or group who serves in each branch and 2) one of the duties each branch has.

Word Bank

governor

courts

makes laws

rules on laws

General Assembly

makes sure laws carried out

LEGISLATIVE BRANCH
1) _____
2) _____

EXECUTIVE BRANCH
1) _____
2) _____

JUDICIAL BRANCH
1) _____
2) _____

Enrichment Exercise

For each of these government offices, circle whether it is part of the EXECUTIVE, the LEGISLATIVE, or the JUDICIAL branch.

1.	District Attorney	EXECUTIVE	LEGISLATIVE	JUDICIAL
2.	Senator	EXECUTIVE	LEGISLATIVE	JUDICIAL
3.	Governor	EXECUTIVE	LEGISLATIVE	JUDICIAL
4.	Supreme Court of Appeals	EXECUTIVE	LEGISLATIVE	JUDICIAL
5.	Delegate	EXECUTIVE	LEGISLATIVE	JUDICIAL
6.	Circuit Court Judge	EXECUTIVE	LEGISLATIVE	JUDICIAL
7.	State Treasurer	EXECUTIVE	LEGISLATIVE	JUDICIAL
8.	General Assembly	EXECUTIVE	LEGISLATIVE	JUDICIAL
9.	Supreme Court Justice	EXECUTIVE	LEGISLATIVE	JUDICIAL
10.	Lieutenant Governor	EXECUTIVE	LEGISLATIVE	JUDICIAL

One More — Just For Fun!

Here are some examples of old Virginia laws:

• *No playing marbles for keeps.*
• *You can't own a cat and a bird at the same time.*
• *No working in bare feet.*
• *You cannot sleep in someone's outhouse without permission.*
• *Citizens must honk their horns while passing other cars.*
• *Children are not to go trick-or-treating on Halloween.*

What do you think? Have you ever broken any of these laws?

A Quick Review For You!

1. Who is the head of Virginia's executive branch?

    A. The president

    B. The governor

    C. A Supreme Court justice

2. Which branch is the General Assembly a part of?

    A. Legislative

    B. Judicial

    C. Executive

3. Which branch makes sure that the laws are carried out?

    A. Legislative

    B. Judicial

    C. Executive

4. Which branch is the state's court system?

    A. Legislative

    B. Judicial

    C. Executive

5. Which branch decides whether or not a law agrees with Virginia's constitution?

    A. Legislative

    B. Judicial

    C. Executive

6. What is the name for the power each branch holds over the others?

    A. Duplex and checks

    B. Checks and balances

    C. Balance beam

A Productive State!

Products

product: something that has been made in order to sell it

Different products characterize each of Virginia's five regions. Here are some of the major products of each region of Virginia:

- *Coastal Plain (Tidewater) — Seafood*
- *Piedmont — Tobacco products, information technology*
- *Blue Ridge Mountains — Apples*
- *Valley and Ridge — Poultry, apples*
- *Appalachian Plateau — Coal*

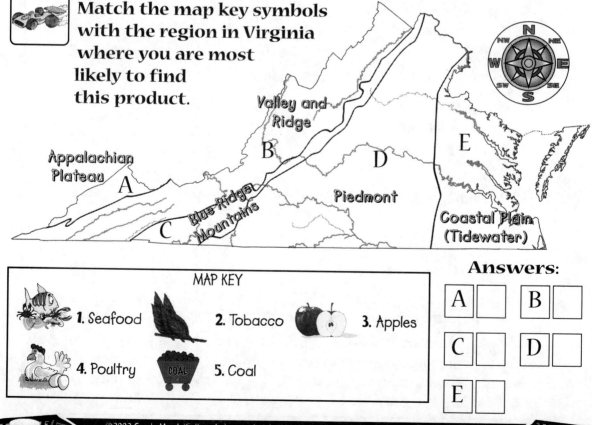

Match the map key symbols with the region in Virginia where you are most likely to find this product.

MAP KEY

1. Seafood
2. Tobacco
3. Apples
4. Poultry
5. Coal

Answers:

A ☐   B ☐
C ☐   D ☐
E ☐

Industries

Different industries characterize each of Virginia's five regions. Here are some of the major industries of each region in Virginia.

industry: organized economic activity connected with the production of a particular product

- *Coastal Plain (Tidewater) — Shipbuilding, tourism, federal military installations*
- *Piedmont — Technology, federal and state government, farming, textiles*
- *Blue Ridge Mountains — Recreation*
- *Valley and Ridge — Farming*
- *Appalachian Plateau — Coal Mining*

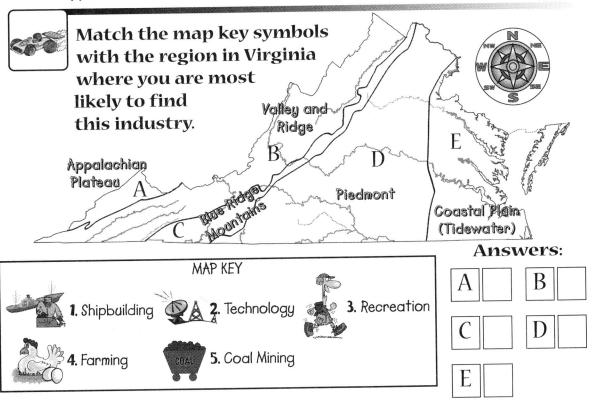

Match the map key symbols with the region in Virginia where you are most likely to find this industry.

MAP KEY

1. Shipbuilding
2. Technology
3. Recreation
4. Farming
5. Coal Mining

Answers:

A ☐   B ☐
C ☐   D ☐
E ☐

The product or industry that each region is characterized by depends on the different regions. Virginia's waterways and natural harbors encouraged the Coastal Plain (Tidewater) seafood and shipbuilding industry. The state's temperate climate and fertile soil helped develop the state's farm crops. The climate in the Piedmont region is good for growing tobacco. The soil and weather patterns are good for growing apples in the Blue Ridge Mountains and in the Valley and Ridge

regions. Because of natural coal deposits, coal mining is important in the Appalachian Plateau. Many of Virginia's important products are natural resources.

natural resources: things that exist in or are formed by nature

Weather Report!

*Match the weather forecasts with the person it will **hurt** most!*

A. hurricane!   1. farmers
B. no rain   2. fishermen

*Match the weather forecasts with the person it will **help** most!*

A. sunny and warm   1. farmers
B. gentle rain   2. tour guide

A Quick Review For You!

1. Virginia's waterways and natural _____ encouraged the Coastal Plain (Tidewater) seafood and shipbuilding industry.

2. The state's temperate _____ and fertile _____ helped develop the state's farm crops.

3. A natural resource found beneath the Appalachian Plateau: _____

4. What is a crop that is well suited to Virginia's climate and soil?
   A. Apples   B. Tobacco
   C. A and B   D. neither A nor B

5. Which product was as important to Jamestown settlers as it is to the Piedmont today?
   A. Apples   B. Poultry
   C. Tobacco   D. Coal

6. In what region would you find federal military installations?
   A. Coastal Plain (Tidewater)   B. Blue Ridge Mountains
   C. Appalachian Plateau   D. Piedmont

VS.10c — Advances in transportation, communications, and technology have contributed to Virginia's prosperity and role in the global economy. Correlates with VS.1d and VS.1e.

Virginia On the Move!

In the 20th Century, Virginia saw many advances in transportation and communication. These advances facilitated migration and led to increased economic development.

migration: the movement from one place to another

Industries in Virginia produce goods and services used throughout the United States. Transportation-related improvements have moved raw materials to manufacturing centers and finished products to markets. These improvements include:

- an extensive highway system across the state
- the expansion of railroads
- an increase in airports and airplanes

Using the map below, do the following:

Put an **I** beside a transportation system that lets industries transport their finished products by road.

Put an **R** beside a transportation system that lets the coal industry transport raw materials to Virginia's ports.

Put an **A** beside the transportation system that lets people and goods move most quickly around Virginia, the United States, and the world.

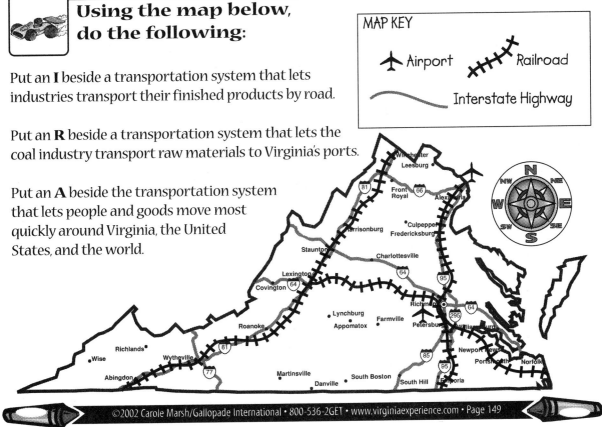

MAP KEY

✈ Airport   Railroad

Interstate Highway

The Bigger Picture!

Virginia is an important part of the U.S. economy. Many people from other places in the United States and from around the world have migrated to Virginia for employment. They work in the state's many industries that produce goods and products. They also work in Virginia's service industries.

Some of the goods that Virginia exports include:

- *manufactured products, including textiles, coal, and ships*
- *agricultural products, including tobacco and poultry*

Services are things that people do for other people that they cannot, or do not want to, do for themselves. Examples of services include dry cleaning, package delivery, and computer repair. Tourism is one of Virginia's largest service industries and is a major part of the state's economy.

Check which people work in Virginia's tourism industry.

☐ Hotel/motel housekeeper   ☐ Airline reservations clerk

☐ Travel agent   ☐ Tour bus driver

☐ Historic site guide   ☐ Airline pilot

Advances in communication systems also helped Virginia achieve greater economic growth. Virginia has one of the greatest concentrations of high-technology industries in the United States.

One More - Just for Fun!

*Tourism is an important Virginia industry. A friend from another state writes and asks you where he should visit in your state and why. On a separate piece of paper, tell him **where** he should go and **why**!*

Mega-what?!

Eastern Virginia is part of the northeast *megalopolis*. The northeast megalopolis is a string of urbanized areas extending along the Atlantic Coast from Boston south to the Hampton Roads area. Virginia became a part of this megalopolis because of its extensive economic development.

Draw a line from one end of the northeast megalopolis to the other, going through the major cities.
Draw a circle around the nation's capital.
Draw a star on the capital of Virginia.

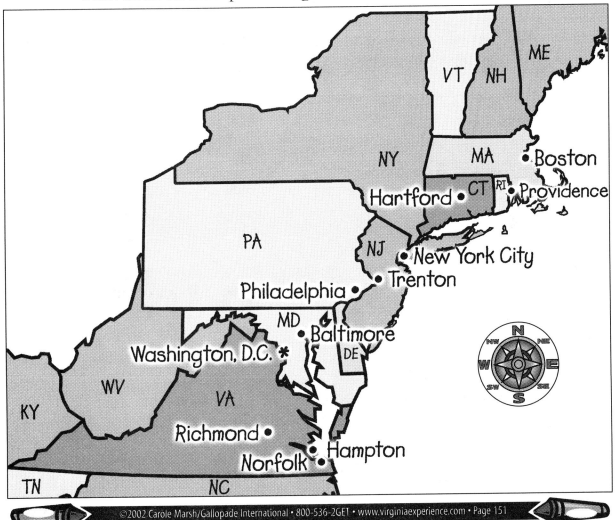

The federal government has a significant impact on Virginia's economy. Many Virginians are employed by the federal government in the Washington, D.C. metropolitan area. Federal military installations employ many people in the Hampton Roads area.

metropolitan area : a city and its surrounding developed area

Can you identify these people and their jobs?

Put an **A** by the person involved in Virginia's shipbuilding industry.

Put a **B** by the people working at a military installation.

Put a **C** by the person working at a federal government office.

You have a friend who lives in California. She is studying Virginia, too.

Write her a letter describing some of the changes in communications, transportation, or technology during the course of Virginia's history.

_____

_____

_____

_____

_____

_____

_____

_____

_____

_____

_____

Hard to Believe But True!

• *Visitors can still see evidence of prehistoric giant landslides today in the Jefferson National Forest, near Roanoke. One landslide is more than THREE MILES LONG! Wow!*

• *Virginia's largest natural lake, Lake Drummond in the Great Dismal Swamp, may have been created by a meteor.*

• *Prehistoric fossils of snails, shells, corals, and other creatures can be seen in the black limestone squares of the capitol's checkerboard floors. They are estimated to be 400 to 450 million years old!*

Virginia X-Files:
- Lynchburg, 1830s: newspapers reported strange happenings: an earthquake, a hailstorm, a meteor storm, and spooky lights in the sky!
- Norfolk, 1853: newspapers reported that during a hailstorm, catfish fell from the sky!

Here are some websites to help you learn more about Virginia!

The Virginia Experience! — http://www.virginiaexperience.com

Virginia Government — http://www.state.va.us

Virginia Travel — http://www.virginia.org

Virginia Facts and Figures — http://www.vipnet.org

Life in Colonial Williamsburg — http://www.history.org

Thomas Jefferson — http://www.monticello.org

George Washington — http://www.mountvernon.org

The American Civil War — http://www.americancivilwar.com

Hard to Believe But True!

George Washington was the first man to sign the U.S. Constitution as presiding officer of the 1787 Constitutional Convention in Philadelphia.

Section 6

Extra Credit

Do You Speak the Language?

Using the word bank below, see if you can translate the paragraph from "Old English" to today's English!

balloo - a game of ball
costardmonger - apple seller
mammothrept - spoiled child
strummel patched - long, loose, tangled hair

Old English

After the children finished their lessons and chores, they would go outside to play balloo. They played balloo in the street, and often knocked down the costardmonger. Whenever Sam lost the game, he would act like a mammothrept. And Molly would be scolded by her mother for coming home with strummel patched.

Today's English

_____

_____

_____

_____

_____

_____

_____

_____

_____

_____

Houses the early Virginia colonists built were simple structures for protection against the weather and attacks. They were made of materials at hand, such as mud and rough wood. Later, as bigger and fancier buildings were constructed in Williamsburg, the colonists copied ideas from the homes back in England. Some of these buildings were made of brick and wood. We still see examples of English architecture in America today.

Using the diagrams below, answer the following questions.

1. Early colonists' houses were for protection

against _____ and _____.

2. Houses built later were copied from homes back in _____.

3. Buildings in Williamsburg were made of _____ and _____.

```
           Early
         Colonists'
          Houses
```

| Simple structures | Made of mud and rough wood | Protection from weather and attacks |

```
         Colonists'
        Houses Built
           Later
```

| Bigger and fancier | Made of brick and wood | Copied from homes in England |

Wonderful Words!

Find the words from the Word Bank in the puzzle below.

Word Bank

barter	government	secession
coal	Indians	slaves
colony	Jefferson	tobacco
England	Lee	Virginia
freedom	Monroe	Washington

```
C O Q J E F F E R S O N N P R
O C O W B O Z M O D E E R F I
A L K J S C B E R T Y W Q X Y
L I C O T O B A C C O E R B N
L N I Q X L W D R U Y V Z Q T
I D B P T O C N L T U W C B N
V I R G I N I A O E E C O M Q
I A O X C Y R L Z W O R B O I
C N Q W O T M G O P Y U M N E
C S G O V E R N M E N T U R Z
C O L A S D O E M O P W H O Q
C P W A S H I N G T O N M E I
O W E I V O E V C X Z Y U I O
Z O V L E E X W Y Z R T S D F
N B C O E X S E C E S S I O N
```

More Wonderful Words!

Imagine that you are writing a letter to someone who has never been to Virginia. Fill in the blanks with your own words.

Dear _____,

      Please come visit me in Virginia! I think you would have a lot of fun visiting _____ (my town). Since I live in the _____ Region, we would find _____ and _____ nearby. My favorite time of year in Virginia is _____ (season), because _____. If you want to travel around the state, we could visit _____ and _____ (places I've been before).

Sincerely,

_____

Tumultuous Timelines!

Put the following events in the correct sequence on the timeline below by numbering them.

1600

☐ ERA OF MASSIVE RESISTANCE

☐ DECLARATION OF INDEPENDENCE WRITTEN

☐ CONSTITUTIONAL CONVENTION

☐ SETTLING OF JAMESTOWN

☐ CHARTERS OF THE VIRGINIA COMPANY OF LONDON

☐ WILLIAMSBURG BECOMES THE COLONIAL CAPITAL

☐ FIRST REPRESENTATIVE ASSEMBLY IN THE NEW WORLD

☐ CIVIL WAR BEGINS

☐ CIVIL WAR ENDS - SLAVES ARE FREED

☐ RICHMOND BECOMES VIRGINIA'S CAPITAL

☐ FIRST BLACK GOVERNOR ELECTED IN VIRGINIA

PRESENT

Scavenger Hunt!

Use the information on the listed pages to find the answers to these questions. . .

Page #   Question

23   What group of Indians lived in the Piedmont region?

_____

33   Why did England want to establish an American colony?

_____

58   Where did the Scotch-Irish and Germans settle?

_____

73   Why did conflict develop between the colonies and England?

_____

83   Who wrote the Declaration of Independence?

_____

101   What does the word "culture" mean?

_____

111   What were the issues fought over during the Civil War?

_____

147   What type of industry is found in southwestern Virginia?

_____

75   What is a boycott?

_____

143   Who is the head of the executive branch in state government?

_____

~ This book is not reproducible. ~

Early American Food Trivia

Below are some foods that Virginians ate long ago (and still eat today — but some are not named the same). Can you match the food with its definition?

1. Succotash _____   A. a form of beaten biscuits

2. Marmalade _____   B. a thick soup made with clams, fish and vegetables

3. Fool _____   C. pan gravy made from fried ham

4. Shoofly Pie _____   D. juice made from apples or other fruit

5. Punch _____   E. ankle of a pig

6. Spoon bread _____   F. a loaf or oval-shaped bread or cake

7. Hoppin' John _____   G. salad

8. Salat _____   H. a dish made with black-eyed peas, rice, and salt pork or bacon

9. Apoquinimine Cakes _____   I. a dish made of corn and beans

10. Pone _____   J. a baked dish made of cornmeal, eggs, and shortening

11. Chowder _____   K. jelly or preserves with small pieces of fruit or rind in it

12. Red-eye gravy _____   L. an English dessert made of crushed, cooked fruit and cream or custard

13. Cider _____   M. pie filled with a mixture of flour, butter, brown sugar, and molasses

14. Ham Hock _____   N. a drink made with two or more fruit juices, sugar, spices, and water

What Did You Sayeth?!

Below are some Old English words that Virginians spoke long ago. Write a short story using some of these words . . .

Arn - iron • Balloo - a game of ball • Costardmonger - apple seller
Crevise - lobster • Dibble - moustache • Frumety - oatmeal
Luzarne - bobcat or mountain lion
Mammothrept - spoiled child • Openauk - potato
Piddle-diddle - procrastinate • Seekanauk - king or horseshoe crab
Shot Sharks - underwear • Strummel Patched - long, loose, tangled hair
Weroance - Indian chief

_____

_____

_____

_____

_____

_____

_____

_____

_____

_____

_____

_____

_____

_____

_____

_____

_____

_____

_____

Fill-In Crossword

Let's visit the regions again! Fill in the blank crossword with the names of the four regions and their unique characteristics. We've given you one to start from.

Coastal Plain
Tidewater
Seafood
Tourism

Piedmont
Peanuts
Tobacco

Valley and Ridge
Farming
Poultry

Blue Ridge Mountains
Apples
Recreation

Appalachian Plateau
Coal

V
I
R
G
I
N
I
A
R
E
G
I
O
N
S

Virginia Studies Practice Test

1. In which region did the Powhatan Indians live?
    A   Piedmont
    B   Coastal Plain (Tidewater)
    C   Valley and Ridge
    D   Appalachian Plateau

2. Where did the Scotch-Irish and Germans settle?
    F   Near the James River
    G   Near the Pacific Ocean
    H   In the Shenandoah Valley
    J   In the Blue Ridge Mountains

3. On what river was Richmond founded?
    A   The Potomac River
    B   The James River
    C   The Chesapeake River
    D   The New River

4. Which of the following states does not form part of Virginia's border?
    F   Texas
    G   West Virginia
    H   Kentucky
    J   North Carolina

5. Which industry became important in the Coastal Plain (Tidewater) region?
    A   Lumbering
    B   Coal mining
    C   Poultry farming
    D   Ship building

6. In what region is coal mined?
    F   Appalachian Plateau
    G   Valley and Ridge
    H   Piedmont
    J   Tidewater

7. Which of these areas has low population density?
    A   Richmond
    B   Northern Virginia
    C   Eastern Shore
    D   Virginia Beach

8. In what region would you find farming, technology, federal and state government, and the textile industries?
    F   Blue Ridge Mountains
    G   Valley and Ridge
    H   Piedmont
    J   Appalachian Plateau

9. Into how many regions is Virginia divided?
    A   Four
    B   Five
    C   Six
    D   Seven

10. Which of the following was the first representative assembly in America?
    F   Congress
    G   General Court
    H   House of Burgesses
    J   House of Representatives

11. What type of government did the Virginia colony have?
    A Representative
    B Monarchy
    C Communist
    D Socialist

12. Which of the following groups did NOT contribute to the development of the Virginia colony?
    F German settlers
    G Migrant workers
    H African slaves
    J American Indians

13. How did colonists buy goods and services in colonial Virginia?
    A They bartered
    B They used coins
    C They wrote checks
    D They used credit cards

14. Which of the following was not a reason for the start of the Civil War?
    F The color of the national flag
    G States' rights
    H Slavery
    J The preservation of the Union

15. Who commanded the Confederate Army?
    A Ulysses S. Grant
    B Jefferson Davis
    C Thomas Jackson
    D Robert E. Lee

16. What were the years after the Civil War called?
    F Massive Resistance
    G Reconstruction
    H Rebuilding Time
    J Civil Rights Era

17. What were the laws that discriminated against African-Americans called?
    A John Doe laws
    B Equal Rights laws
    C Jim Crow laws
    D Integration laws

18. What happened to Virginia's cities after Reconstruction?
    F They became more violent
    G They became less safe
    H They got smaller
    J They began to grow

19. Which of the following is NOT a type of service provided by the government?
    A Massages
    B Public schools
    C Police and fire departments
    D Interstate highways

20. Which of the following made it difficult for African Americans to vote after Reconstruction?
    F New roads
    G Poll taxes
    H Better education
    J Better farming techniques

Virginia Studies
Practice Test 2

1. Who were the first people who lived in Virginia?
   A Scotch, Irish and Germans
   B English settlers
   C American Indians
   D Black slaves

2. Where did the English make their first settlement?
   F Appalachian Plateau
   G In the Shenandoah Valley
   H On the Potomac River
   J At the mouth of the James River

3. Which of these cities developed along the Potomac River?
   A Alexandria
   B Roanoke
   C Richmond
   D Williamsburg

4. Why did cities develop in the Shenandoah Valley?
   F Natural harbor
   G Along the migration route
   H Shipbuilding was important
   J Fishing was good

5. Who led the Massive Resistance movement against integration of public schools in Virginia?
   A Woodrow Wilson
   B Arthur Ashe
   C Harry F. Byrd, Sr.
   D Dr. Martin Luther King, Jr.

6. What crop is grown in the Valley and Ridge region?
   F Tobacco
   G Coal
   H Apples
   J Cotton

7. What type of industry is found in the Blue Ridge Mountains?
   A Recreation
   B Textile factories
   C Lumbering
   D Coal mining

8. What type of industry is found in the Appalachian Plateau?
   F Lumbering
   G Coal mining
   H Shipbuilding
   J Poultry farming

9. Which of the following products can be found in the Coastal Plain (Tidewater)?
   A A harbor
   B Orchards and caverns
   C Coal mines
   D Seafood

10. What type of land is found in the Piedmont region?
   F Coastal plain
   G Rolling hills
   H Large rocky mountains
   J High plains

11. Which region of Virginia is next to the Atlantic Ocean?
    A   Coastal Plain (Tidewater)
    B   Great Plains
    C   Basin and Ridge
    D   Coastal Range

12. Why did conflict develop between England and the Virginia colony?
    F   Virginia could not export a successful crop to England
    G   Taxation and lack of representation in government
    H   Many people wanted to leave England for Virginia
    J   Sickness in Virginia

13. Why did the Virginia Company of London establish the Virginia colony?
    A   To get rid of English prisoners
    B   To find a passage to Asia
    C   To make money
    D   To help the English king

14. How did American Indians help Virginia colonists?
    F   Taught them survival strategies
    G   Inexpensive source of labor
    H   Taught the colonists' children
    J   Sold them lumber to build

15. Which of the following was a highly valued barter item in colonial Virginia?
    A   Seashells
    B   Credit cards
    C   Baseball cards
    D   Tobacco

16. Which of the following events did Virginians participate in that led to war between the colonies and England?
    F   The War of 1812
    G   Continental Congresses
    H   The Warsaw Pact
    J   Wars with Indians

17. Who wrote the Declaration of Independence?
    A   Thomas Jefferson
    B   James Monroe
    C   George Mason
    D   James Madison

18. Who is known as the "Father of Our Country"?
    F   George Mason
    G   James Madison
    H   Patrick Henry
    J   George Washington

19. Who said, "Give me liberty or give me death"?
    A   George Mason
    B   James Madison
    C   Patrick Henry
    D   George Washington

20. Who wrote the Virginia Declaration of Rights?
    F   Benjamin Franklin
    G   George Mason
    H   Thomas Jefferson
    J   George Wythe

Virginia Studies Practice Test 3

1. Why are the Charters of the Virginia Company of London significant?
   A Formed the basis for the Declaration of Independence
   B Allowed colonists to keep profits
   C Guaranteed freedom of religion
   D Extended English rights to colonists

2. Which document formed the basis of the Bill of Rights?
   F Virginia Statute for Religious Freedom
   G Declaration of Independence
   H Virginia Declaration of Rights
   J Articles of Confederation

3. Which amendment guarantees freedom of religion?
   A The First amendment
   B The Second Amendment
   C The Third Amendment
   D The Fifth Amendment

4. What is the Declaration of Independence?
   F Explains why the colonies should stay part of England
   G Gave colonists the rights of Englishmen
   H Guaranteed freedom of religion
   J Explained why the colonies should break away from England

5. Who was president of the Constitutional Convention?
   A George Mason
   B George Washington
   C James Madison
   D Patrick Henry

6. Who is known as the "Father of the Constitution"?
   F George Mason
   G George Washington
   H James Madison
   J Patrick Henry

7. Who authorized the purchase of the Louisiana Territory?
   A George Washington
   B James Madison
   C Benjamin Franklin
   D Thomas Jefferson

8. What did abolitionists in the United States want to do away with?
   F Slavery
   G Drinking
   H Tobacco
   J Stealing

9. Which part of Virginia was opposed to slavery before the Civil War?
   A The eastern counties
   B People in the Tidewater region
   C The western counties
   D People who owned slaves

10. What kind of economy did the South have before the Civil War?
    F   Heavy industrial
    G   Agricultural
    H   Light industrial
    J   Dependent on the sea

11. Who seized the federal arsenal at Harpers Ferry in an attempt to arm slaves?
    A   Jefferson Davis
    B   Nat Turner
    C   John Brown
    D   Abraham Lincoln

12. Who led a slave revolt against plantation owners in Virginia?
    F   Nat Turner
    G   Harriet Tubman
    H   John Brown
    J   Robert E. Lee

13. What state was formed when the western counties of Virginia broke away before the Civil War?
    A   Kentucky
    B   Tennessee
    C   Maryland
    D   West Virginia

14. What city in Virginia was the capital of the Confederacy?
    F   Washington
    G   Richmond
    H   Yorktown
    J   Williamsburg

15. Where was the first battle of the Civil War fought?
    A   Gettysburg
    B   Lexington
    C   Manassas
    D   Fredericksburg

16. Which of the following is a way to protest discrimination?
    F   Massive Resistance
    G   Prejudice
    H   Segregation
    J   Boycotts and sit-ins

17. What did Congress do to help newly freed slaves after the Civil War?
    A   Built them new homes
    B   Created the Freedman's Bureau
    C   Gave them money to buy food
    D   Nothing

18. What type of service does the state government provide?
    F   Interstate highways
    G   Local streets
    H   State colleges and universities
    J   National defense

19. Who opened the first bank for African Americans?
    A   Maggie Lena Walker
    B   Susan B. Anthony
    C   Jane Addams
    D   Booker T. Washington

Section 7

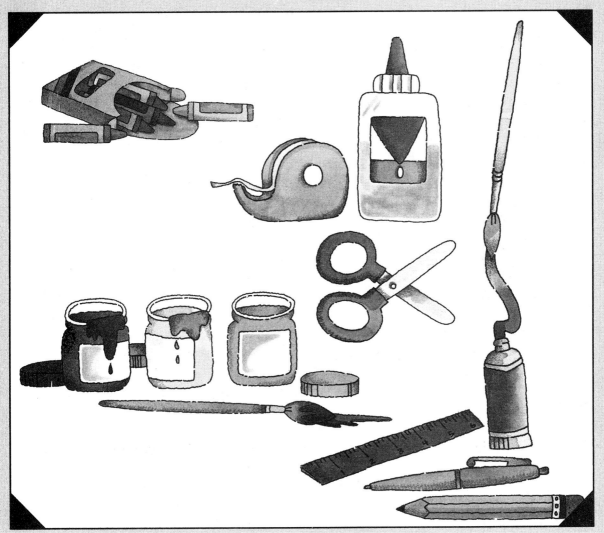

Appendix

VIRGINIA

~ 9500 BC
Paleo (ancient) people inhabit Virginia

1492 AD
Christopher Columbus discovers America

1607
104 English colonists establish a settlement at Jamestown

1619
House of Burgesses formed; first Africans brought to Virginia

1624
Virginia becomes a royal British colony

1644
Peace treaty with Powhatan Indians signed

1649
Slavery is practiced in Virginia

1676
Nathaniel Bacon's Rebellion against the governor

1693
College of William and Mary is chartered

1699
Capital is moved to Williamsburg (Middle Plantation)

1775
Revolutionary War begins

1776
Declaration of Independence from England is signed

1780
Richmond becomes capital

1781
British surrender at Yorktown

1786
Virginia Statute for Religious Freedom is adopted

1788
Virginia becomes the 10th American state

1789
George Washington becomes first U.S. president

1800
Slave Gabriel leads revolt

TIMELINE

1801
Thomas Jefferson becomes America's third president

1831
Nat Turner's Rebellion against slavery

1859
John Brown raids Harpers Ferry

1861
Virginia secedes from the Union; Civil War starts

1865
Robert E. Lee surrenders at Appomattox; Civil War ends

1870
Virginia is readmitted to the Union

1914
Virginians serve in World War I

1920
Virginia women get the right to vote

1941
Virginians serve in World War II

1959
Virginia schools begin to integrate

1964
Civil Rights Act is passed

1965
Virginians serve in Vietnam War

1988
Virginia celebrates its bicentennial

1989
Virginia elects first African-American governor in the nation, L. Douglas Wilder

1999
Virginia students on the Internet

2001
Virginia enters the 21st Century

WHAT IS IN VIRGINIA'S FUTURE??

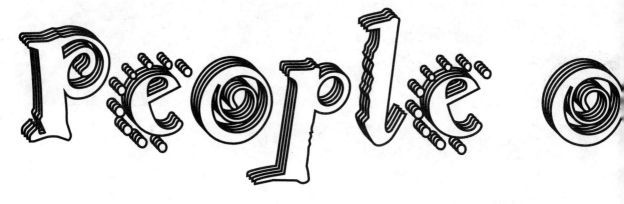

People

Colonial and Revolutionary War Eras

Nathaniel Bacon, a young plantation owner, led a rebellion against the colonial government in Virginia in 1676. He claimed the government did not protect farmers from Indian raids, led other farmers in attacks against the Indians, and captured and burned the city of Jamestown.

George Rogers Clark, a Revolutionary War soldier born near Charlottesville, helped win battles that extended U.S. territories far to the west.

William Clark was born in Caroline County. He was part of the expedition that included Meriwether Lewis and was sent to explore the Louisiana Territory.

"I have not yet begun to fight!" cried **John Paul Jones**, a Fredericksburg naval officer, when the British demanded he surrender during a 1779 Revolutionary War battle.

Francis Lightfoot Lee, Richard Henry Lee's brother, was a member of the House of Burgesses, signed the Declaration of Independence, and was a delegate to the First Continental Congress.

"Light-Horse Harry" Lee, born near Dumfries, was a great cavalry commander during the American Revolution. He was a member of the Continental Congress, served as governor of Virginia and a as member of the House of Representatives.

Richard Henry Lee was a political leader in colonial Virginia. He signed the Declaration of Independence, served in the Continental Congress, and was a U.S. Senator.

Meriwether Lewis, born in Albemarle County, explored the Louisiana Purchase with William Clark.

Much legend has grown up around the life of the Indian princess **Pocahontas**. The fact is that she was the daughter of the Indian chief Powhatan when the first settlers came to Virginia. She was the first Indian in the New World converted to Christianity. She married John Rolfe and traveled with him to England. Sadly, she died when she was only 22 years old.

Even less is known about **Chief Powhatan** than his legendary daughter. It is said that he ruled over about 9,000 Indians in what is now eastern Virginia. He tried to keep the peace with the English settlers, but it must have been difficult for him to see his people's native lands gradually taken away by the white colonists. After he died, relations between the Indians and whites grew worse until the Indians were completely forced off their lands.

Without the efforts of **Sir Walter Raleigh**, Virginia may never have been settled. He organized several voyages to the New World, including the famous Lost Colony. He gave Virginia its name but never set foot on its shores himself.

The husband of the Indian princess Pocahontas, **John Rolfe,** made an important contribution to Virginia's future by developing a sweeter-smelling tobacco that was popular in England. Without this cash crop, Virginia would not have become a leading British colony and the successful state it is today.

Without **Captain John Smith,** the Jamestown colony would not have survived. As a member of the first group of settlers, he tried to get along with the Indians, even learning their language. He forced the settlers to work hard and spent a lot of time exploring and mapping the Atlantic coast.

Civil War Era

An ardent abolitionist, **John Brown** led a raid on Harpers Ferry (now part of West Virginia) in 1859 in an attempt to free the slaves through armed force. His raid was stopped by the U.S. military, but it had the effect of increasing tension between the North and the South before the Civil War.

One of the greatest and most famous Confederate Civil War generals, **Thomas "Stonewall" Jackson,** was born in Clarksburg and nicknamed "Stonewall" for his firm stance during battle.

Born a slave in Southampton County, **Nat Turner** led a slave rebellion in 1831 in which nearly 60 people were killed. The rebellion led to stricter slave codes in the South.

Musical Virginians

Pearl Bailey was born in Newport News. As a singer and actress, she won a Tony Award and was a frequent guest at the White House. She won the Medal of Freedom in 1988 for her commitment to her country.

Alvin Pleasant Carter, born in Maces Spring, formed the Carter Family singers, who recorded more than 300 mountain, folk, and country music songs.

Patsy Cline was born in Gore during the Great Depression. She was the first female country singer to break into the pop music charts. Two of her best-known hits are *I Fall to Pieces* and *Crazy*.

Ella Fitzgerald, born in Newport News, was the first female singer to develop a jazz-style voice. She became famous for singing in a "scat" style and performed all over the world with well-known musicians.

Bill "Bojangles" Robinson, born in Richmond, is honored each year with National Tap Dance Day.

Kate Smith of Greenville became known as the "first lady of radio" and was famous for singing "God Bless America."

Soprano **Camilla Williams**, from Danville, was the first African American to sing a major role at the Vienna State Opera, in 1954, in *Madame Butterfly*.

Scientific Virginians

Richard Byrd, born in Winchester, was one of the first two people to fly over the North Pole in 1926. He later explored the Arctic and Antarctic.

Hampton's **Katherine Johnson**, a mathematician and NASA scientist, used pencil and paper to do the algebra for the Alan Shepard flight, the John Glenn orbit, and the 1969 Apollo moon mission.

Sarah Garland Jones was the first African American and the first woman to be certified by the Virginia State Board of Medicine. In 1895, she and her husband co-founded Richmond Community Hospital.

Inventor of the reaper, **Cyrus McCormick** of Rockbridge County helped revolutionize farming in Virginia and the nation!

Belroi-born **Walter Reed** was an army doctor who helped save lives when he discovered how the diseases typhoid and yellow fever were spread through mosquito bites!

Booker T. Washington, born near Roanoke, helped Tuskegee Institute to become a leading center of black education.

Carter G. Woodson, born in Buckingham County in 1875, founded Negro History Week, now Black History Month, to celebrate the achievements of African Americans.

Political Virginians

William Henry Harrison, born in Charles City County, was the 9th President. He died of pneumonia after serving only one month in office.

George Marshall of Uniontown was awarded the 1953 Nobel Peace Prize for his role in helping to rebuild Europe after World War II.

Judge **John Marshall**, born near Germantown (now Midland), helped build the U.S. Supreme Court into a strong and equal branch of the federal government.

Zachary Taylor, born in Orange County, was the 12th president of the U.S. He was known as "Old Rough and Ready."

John Tyler was William Henry Harrison's vice-president and took over the presidency after Harrison's death. He was born in Charles City County and served as governor of Virginia and a U.S. senator before becoming vice president.

Literary Virginians

Anne Beattie, a resident of Charlottesville, has won numerous awards and distinctions for her early stories published in *New Yorker* and her subsequent novels.

Willa Cather, born near Winchester, is best known for her novels, *O Pioneers!* and *My Antonia*, which she wrote based on her experiences migrating west with her family.

Virginius Dabney was an award-winning editor of the *Richmond Times-Dispatch* from 1936–1969.

Contemporary author **Annie Dillard** received a Pulitzer Prize in 1975 for *Pilgrim at Tinker Creek*, about life in the Roanoke River Valley.

With little formal education but by being a voracious reader, **Ellen Glasgow** became such an excellent writer about Virginia that her book, *In This Our Life*, won a Pulitzer Prize in 1942.

Many young Americans learned to read from **William McGuffey's** "Readers" in the late 1800s and early 1900s.

Edgar Allan Poe, raised in Richmond, was a popular short story writer who is still read by people who want a good scare!

Athletic Virginians

Eppa Rixey, born in Culpeper in 1891, was the first Virginian elected to the Baseball Hall of Fame, in 1963. He pitched in 21 seasons and won 266 games for the Philadelphia Phillies and the Cincinnati Reds from 1912 through 1933.

Hot Springs' **Sam Snead** was a hot pro golfer, winning more than 100 tournaments, some on the world's most challenging links!

Piratical Virginians?

Known as "the fiercest pirate of them all," **Blackbeard** (real name: Ned Teach, Edward Thatch, or something similar) was once a regular visitor to Virginia's shores. After he was caught and decapitated, his head was hung on a pole along the Hampton River, at a place called Blackbeard's Point.

Virginia Basic Facts

Nicknames: Old Dominion, Mother of Presidents, Mother of States

State Motto: Sic Semper Tyrannis (Thus Always to Tyrants)

Area: 42,326 square miles; 35th in the nation

VIRGINIA
Old Dominion

State Tree:

Flowering dogwood

State Insect:

Tiger Swallowtail Butterfly

Record low temperature:
-30° F (-34° C) at Mountain Lake Bio Station

Record high temperature:
110° F (43° C) at Columbia

State Bird: Cardinal

State Dog: American foxhound

State Capital: Richmond

State Flower: Dogwood

Highest Elevation: Mount Rogers, at 5,729 feet (1,746 meters)

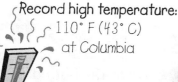

Lowest Elevation: Sea Level

Government:
2 U.S. senators, 11 U.S. representatives.

State Fish: Brook trout

State Drink: Milk

State Shell: Oyster

Legislative body: General Assembly – 40 senators, 100 representatives. 95 counties.

Gazetteer

This page will help you find the places mentioned in the Fourth Grade Student Workbook.

Appalachian Mountains: low, rounded mountains that run along the western edge of Virginia

Appalachian Plateau: found in the southwestern corner of Virginia; consists of a plateau and valuable coal deposits

Atlantic Ocean: the large body of water that borders the United States on the east

Blue Ridge Mountains: old rounded mountains located between the Piedmont and Valley and Ridge regions

Chesapeake Bay: body of water that separates the mainland of Virginia from the Eastern Shore

Coastal Plain (Tidewater): the region of Virginia next to the Atlantic Ocean; a coastal plain

Delmarva Peninsula: peninsula formed by Delaware, part of Maryland, and the Eastern Shore of Virginia

Eastern Shore: a peninsula east of mainland Virginia

Great Dismal Swamp: large swamp found in southeastern Virginia extending into North Carolina

Hampton Roads: harbor area formed at the mouth of the James River

James River: the longest river wholly within Virginia; runs from the mountains to Hampton Roads

Jamestown: located on a peninsula on the James River, about 34 miles from the mouth of the river

Lake Drummond: found in the Great Dismal Swamp, it is the largest natural lake in Virginia

Piedmont (Land at the foot of the mountains): the region next to the Tidewater region; contains a plateau, rolling hills, rapids, and a fall line

Potomac River: forms the boundary between Virginia and Maryland

Richmond: capital city of Virginia; on the Fall Line and the James River

Valley and Ridge Region: contains the Blue Ridge Mountains, valleys, caverns, and the Shenandoah River

Shenandoah Valley: valley formed by the Shenandoah River; runs between the Shenandoah and Blue Ridge Mountains

Williamsburg: second colonial capital of Virginia; located near Jamestown

Geography Glossary

bay: a part of an ocean, sea, or lake that extends into the land

canal: a waterway built to carry water for navigation or irrigation

cavern: a large cave or natural opening into or under the earth

coast: the land along an ocean or sea

community: a group of people who live in a specific place, share government, and often have a common history

English: people who live in or come from the country of England

European: people who live in or come from the continent of Europe

fall line: the natural boundary between the Piedmont and Coastal Plain regions

harbor: a part of a body of water deep enough to anchor a ship

hill: a rounded, raised landform, that is not as high as a mountain

lake: a body of water completely or almost completely surrounded by land

latitude: imaginary lines that run horizontally (east and west) around the globe (also called parallels)

longitude: imaginary lines that run vertically (north and south) around the globe

mountain: a high, rounded, or pointed landform with steep sides

mountain range: a row or chain of mountains

natural resources: things that exist in or are formed by nature

ocean: one of the earth's four largest bodies of salt water

orchard: a grove of trees that bear fruit

peninsula: a body of land surrounded on three sides by water

plateau: a high land area with a flat top

population density: the average number of people who live in a square mile of land

poultry: chickens, turkeys, ducks, or geese raised for their meat or eggs

rapids: a part of a river where the water flows swiftly and roughly

river: a large stream of water that flows in a natural channel across the land and empties into a lake, ocean, or another river

river mouth: the place where a river empties into a larger body of water

temperate: mild; neither too hot, nor too cold

tributary: a river or stream that flows into a larger river or stream

valley: a long, narrow piece of low land set between mountains or hills

History Glossary

abolition: to do away with something; abolitionists wanted to do away with slavery

barter: to trade one thing for another

charter: a document issued by a government authority

colony: a group of people who leave their native country to form a settlement in a new land

compromise: to settle differences by each side giving up something to the other side

conflict: a fight, battle, or struggle

consumer: a buyer of goods or services

credit: getting something today that you promise to pay for at a later time

debt: something that you owe to someone else

guarantee: to promise, assure, or pledge

patriot: a person who loves, serves, and defends his or her country

resign: to give up or quit, as in to quit your job

secession: to pull away from; to leave

surrender: to give up, as in to give up to an enemy force

statute: a formal rule enacted by a legislature

Glossary of Indian Words and Names

Algonquian (al-gahn-kwee-uhn): language spoken by the Powhatans in Virginia and related to other Indian languages along the Atlantic coast

Cattapeuk: meant "spring"

Chesapeake (ches-a-peak): means "big salt bay"

Chickahominy (chick-a-hom-a-nee): means "crushed corn people"

Cohattayough: meant "summer"

huskanaw: Powhatan initiation into manhood

mamanatowick: title given to the chief Powhatan

Okeus: the Powhatans' most powerful god

Opechancanough: Powhatan's brother, who became weroance after Powhatan's death in 1618

pawcorances: altar stones that stood by people's homes, out in the woods, or at any spot that was significant

peak: a type of bead made from quahog shells used by the Powhatans in trading; also called wampum

Popanow: meant "winter"

Pocahontas (poh-kuh-hahn-tuhs): Daughter of the chief Powhatan; her name means "little playful one"; also called Matoaka

Powhatan (pow-a-tan): name for 1) a chief's empire that covered most of the Virginia coastal plain; 2) the name of the chief of a group of Indians; 3) the name of the town where Powhatan was born; near the falls of the James River; may mean "priest's town" or "town at the falls"

weroance: name given to Powhatan's "commanders," or sub-chiefs

yihakan (yeee-ha-cahn): a Powhatan house

Reference Guide

If you need to get more basic information about Virginia's history, government, economy, etc., here are some good books for you to check out of the library.

America the Beautiful: Virginia, by Sylvia McNair. Childrens Press, 1989.

From Sea to Shining Sea: Virginia, by Dennis B. Fradin. Childrens Press, 1992.

Hello U.S.A.: Virginia, by Karen Sirvaitis. Lerner Publications Company, 1991.

Let's Discover the States, ATLANTIC, District of Columbia• Virginia• West Virginia, by Thomas G. Aylesworth and Virginia L. Aylesworth. Chelsea House Publishers, 1988.

My First Book About Virginia!, by Carole Marsh. Gallopade International, 2002.

Steck-Vaughn Portrait of America: Virginia, by Kathleen Thompson. Steck-Vaughn Company, 1996.

The Virginia Experience, by Carole Marsh. Gallopade International, 2002.

A Map of North America

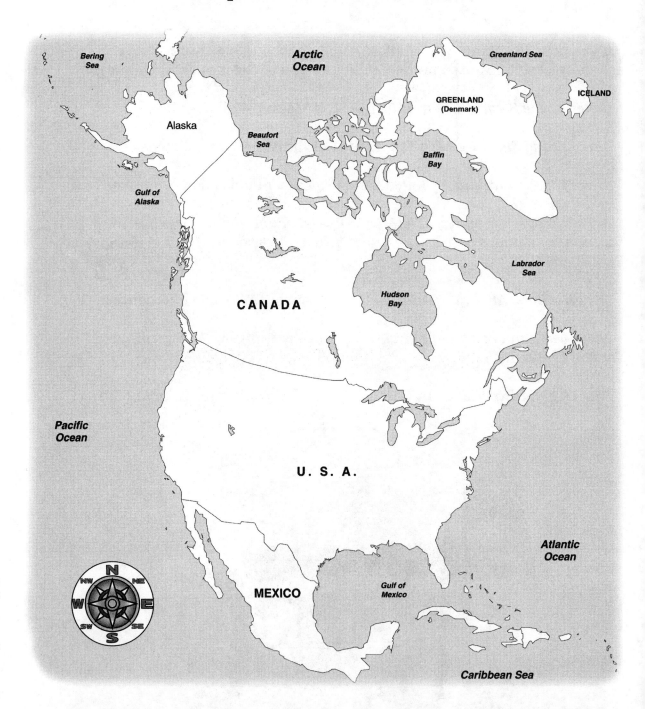

Bering Sea

Arctic Ocean

Greenland Sea

GREENLAND (Denmark)

ICELAND

Alaska

Beaufort Sea

Baffin Bay

Gulf of Alaska

Labrador Sea

CANADA

Hudson Bay

Pacific Ocean

U.S.A.

Atlantic Ocean

N
NW   NE
W   E
SW   SE
S

MEXICO

Gulf of Mexico

Caribbean Sea

A Map of the United States

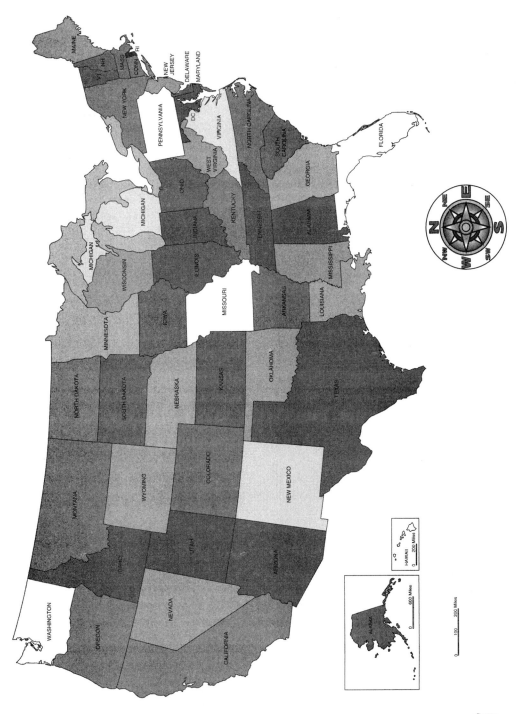

A Map of the 13 Colonies

THE UNITED STATES, 1787

New Hampshire

New York

Massachusetts

Rhode Island

Connecticut

Pennsylvania

New Jersey

Delaware

Maryland

U.S. Territory
(Northwest)

MISSISSIPPI RIVER

OHIO RIVER

Virginia

U.S. Territory

North Carolina

South Carolina

Georgia

N
NW   NE
W   E
SW   SE
S

Virginia's Major Cities

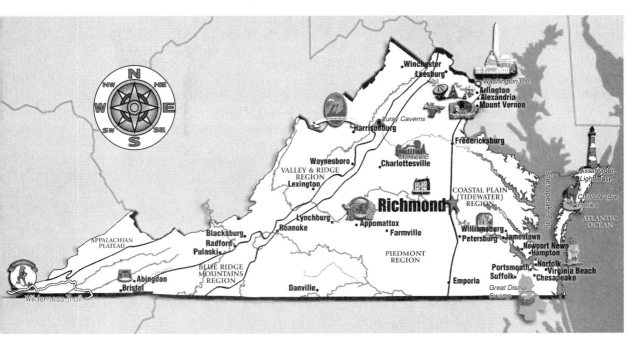

- Winchester
- Leesburg
- Washington D.C.
- Arlington
- Alexandria
- Mount Vernon
- Shenandoah
- Luray Caverns
- Harrisonburg
- Fredericksburg
- Waynesboro
- Monticello
- Charlottesville
- VALLEY & RIDGE REGION
- Lexington
- COASTAL PLAIN (TIDEWATER) REGION
- Richmond
- Lynchburg
- Roanoke
- Appomattox
- Farmville
- APPALACHIAN PLATEAU
- Blacksburg
- Radford
- Pulaski
- Williamsburg
- Petersburg
- Jamestown
- Newport News
- Hampton
- BLUE RIDGE MOUNTAINS REGION
- PIEDMONT REGION
- Portsmouth
- Suffolk
- Norfolk
- Virginia Beach
- Chesapeake
- Abingdon
- Bristol
- Danville
- Emporia
- Great Dismal Swamp
- Wilderness Trail
- Chesapeake Bay
- Assateague Lighthouse
- Chincoteague Ponies
- ATLANTIC OCEAN

Virginia's Rivers & Mountains

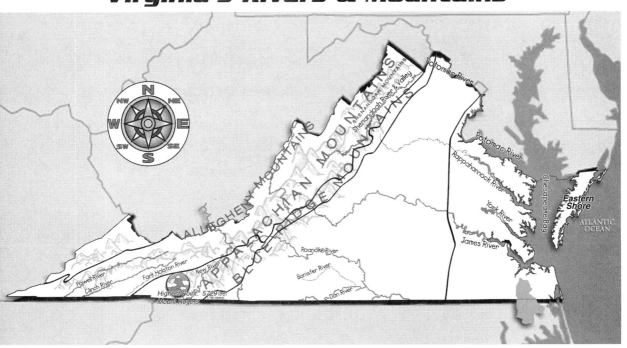

- ALLEGHENY Mountains
- SHENANDOAH MOUNTAINS
- Shenandoah River & Valley
- Potomac River
- Potomac River
- Rappahannock River
- APPALACHIAN MOUNTAINS
- BLUE RIDGE MOUNTAINS
- York River
- James River
- Eastern Shore
- ATLANTIC OCEAN
- Chesapeake Bay
- Roanoke River
- Fork Holston River
- New River
- Banister River
- Powell River
- Clinch River
- Highest Point: 5729 feet (746 meters) Mount Rogers
- Dan River

~ This book is not reproducible. ~

INDEX

Africa 19, 42

African, African American 42, 43, 54, 57, 58, 78, 110, 119, 122, 136, 137, 138, 140, 173, 177, 178

Alexandria 21, 125

American Indians 23, 24, 26, 36, 49, 50, 57, 58, 61

American Revolution 74, 81, 86, 93, 99, 102, 174

Appalachian Plateau 12, 16, 58, 146, 147, 148, 181

architecture 56, 157

Army of Northern Virginia 113

Ashe, Arthur R. 140

Atlantic Ocean 9, 13, 14, 19, 102, 181

banks 67, 69, 70

barter 67, 69, 183

Bill of Rights 85, 94, 95

Blue Ridge Mountains 12, 14, 15, 16, 23, 146, 147, 181

boycott 75, 136

Brown, John 109, 173, 176

Bull Run 113, 114

Byrd, Harry F. 137, 140

catfish 153

caverns 181

Chesapeake Bay 9, 13, 19, 20, 21, 22, 86, 181

civil rights 136, 137

Civil War 111, 113, 114, 115, 116, 117, 118, 125, 126, 154, 173, 176

coal 12, 16, 126, 127, 148, 150, 181

Coastal Plain (Tidewater) 12, 13, 14, 23, 58, 146, 147, 181

compass rose 9

Confederacy 111, 113, 114

credit 69, 183

culture 56, 63, 101

Danville 125, 177

Declaration of Independence 73, 75, 76, 83, 84, 90, 95, 160, 172, 174, 175

desegregation 138

discrimination 122, 137

Eastern Shore 13, 22, 181

Economic Interdependence 34

England 33, 34, 35, 37, 38, 41, 43, 50, 53, 72, 73, 75, 76, 77, 82, 83, 104, 157, 172, 175, 176, 182

Europe, European 11, 19, 33, 34, 35, 43, 53, 101, 178, 182

fall line 13, 14, 21, 181, 182

fashion 41, 104

Freedman's Bureau 119

French 86

French and Indian War 73, 81, 82

General Assembly 39, 143, 180

George Mason 95

Germans 57, 58

Great Valley 15

Hampton 20, 177

Hampton Roads 116, 151, 152, 181

harbor 20, 147, 181, 182

Henry, Patrick 85, 88

House of Burgesses 39, 40, 81, 83, 85, 172, 174

Indentured servants 42, 70

integration 137, 138

Jackson, General Thomas "Stonewall" 113, 114, 176

James River 13, 14, 21, 35, 181, 184

Jamestown 21, 23, 33, 35, 36, 37, 39, 40, 41, 42, 44, 45, 46, 49, 50, 64, 160, 172, 174, 176, 181

Jefferson, Thomas 73, 75, 83, 93, 95, 96, 154, 173

Jim Crow laws 122

John Rolfe 41, 43, 50, 53, 175, 176

language 23, 101, 156, 176, 184

latitude 182

Lee, General Robert E. 113, 114, 173

Lincoln, Abraham 109, 111, 116

longitude 182

Louisiana Purchase 83, 98, 175

Madison, James 94, 95
Manassas 113
Massive Resistance 137, 160
megalopolis 151

Nat Turner 109, 173, 176
natural resources 20, 125, 148, 182
Norfolk 20, 125, 153
Northern Virginia 135

peninsula 13, 21, 22, 35, 181, 182
Piedmont 12, 13, 14, 15, 23, 58, 126, 146, 147,
    181, 182
plantation 42, 54, 58, 70, 109, 118, 119, 174
Pocahontas 49, 50, 175, 176, 184
population density 135, 182
Portsmouth 117
Potomac River 13, 21, 181
Powhatan 23, 45, 48, 49, 50, 172, 175, 184

Reconstruction 118, 122, 125
relative location 9
religion 95, 96
Revolutionary War 77, 78, 86, 89, 107, 174
Richmond 21, 65, 95, 113, 125, 126, 172, 177,
    179, 180, 181

Scotch-Irish 57, 58
Segregation 122, 136, 137, 138
Shenandoah River 15, 181
Shenandoah Valley 58, 181
Slaves 54, 57, 70, 83, 108, 109, 110, 118, 119, 176
Smith, Captain John 45, 46, 48, 49, 176
society 70, 132, 137
Stuart, J.E.B. 114

taxes 72, 73, 85, 122
Tobacco 12, 41, 42, 43, 49, 53, 54, 67, 70, 99, 125,
    126, 146, 147, 150, 176
tourism 12, 147, 150
transportation 19, 20, 21, 125, 127, 132, 149

Valley and Ridge 12, 15, 146, 147, 181
Virginia Company of London 33, 37
Virginia Declaration of Rights 95
Virginia Statute for Religious Freedom 83, 96,
    172

Washington, George 81, 82, 86, 93, 154, 172
Wilder, L. Douglas 140, 173
Winchester 177, 178

Yorktown 20, 21, 77, 86, 87, 172

About the Author...

CAROLE MARSH has been writing about Virginia for more than 20 years. She is the author of the popular Virginia State Stuff series for young readers and creator, along with her son, Michael Marsh, of "Virginia Facts and Factivities," a CD-ROM widely used in Virginia schools. The Byrd side of her family history led the author to spend a great deal of time researching, writing, and making photographs in Virginia. The author of more than 100 Virginia books and other supplementary educational materials, Marsh just completed a new collection of Virginia materials for young people, including a Virginia Pocket Guide for Kids. Marsh correlates her Virginia materials to Virginia's Standards of Learning. Many of her books and other materials have been inspired by or requested by Virginia teachers and librarians.

Note to Teachers

The Answer Key for this workbook is included in *The Virginia Experience for Virginia Studies Teacher Resource Book.* If you did not purchase the Teacher Resource *Book* and need the Answer Key, please call 800-536-2438 and we will fax, mail, or email one to you.